Called and Sent

First published in 2011 by
by New Life Publishing, Luton,
Bedfordshire LU4 9HG

British Library Cataloguing in Publication Data
A catalogue record for this book is available
from the British Library

ISBN 978 1 903623 54 1

Unless otherwise indicated, psalms and canticles are as
quoted in the Divine Office, Collins, London & Glasgow,
1974. Other biblical texts except otherwise stated from
the New American Bible, Devore & Sons Inc., Wichita,
Kansas, 67201. Used with permission.

Typesetting by New Life Publishing,
Luton, UK www.goodnewsbooks.net
Printed and bound in Great Britain

Called and Sent

The Christian Vocation of All the Baptised

Ambrose Walsh

New Life Publishing

for
Mary Anne and James Peter,
first teachers in the way of faith

CONTENTS

Preface

Sharing what we have been given

"Nobody can give away what they do not possess." So says a basic principle of property law. However, people can be entrusted with what does not belong to them with instructions to share it with others. This is what this book is about. The Lord Jesus Christ has said to us, who are his disciples and apostles, "If you cannot be trusted with what is not yours, who will give you what is your very own?"[1]

I first came across the wise adage quoted above 50 years ago when I was a seminarian. We studied Scholastic philosophy and I well remember hearing the saying many times, not as a matter of property law but as a general principle about the way things work. In blunt Latin words, it says, "Nemo dat quod non habet"; and in equally bluff Anglo Saxon: "You can't give what you don't have". That it states the obvious does not make it any the less true. Its wisdom is a salutary warning to all Christians called to share with others their faith in Jesus Christ. In this book, however, I am especially interested in how it applies to people brought up from infancy within the Roman Catholic Church in the United Kingdom.

These days Catholics are being constantly reminded to engage in the Church's mission and in what is spoken of as 'a new evangelisation'. Now that is a turn up for the books, and no mistake! After centuries, when lay people had been led to believe that their role was to "sit up, shut up and pay up" they now find responsibilities being thrust upon them. Where people are ready to shoulder them, some find their way hampered. They can encounter unreformed clerical attitudes and they will surely come against church rules restricting to the clergy responsibilities any Church members could take on.

Some may conclude that this call for engagement in the Church's work is simply because, 'they are short of priests and nuns'. Wrong. On this point we should put the situation in the United Kingdom in perspective. According to figures published for the year 2005, the ratio of priests to people in Brazil (both diocesan and religious priests) was 1:8,630; in France, it was 1:2,039; in the USA, 1:1,439; and in the United Kingdom, 1:847.[2] Official information published at the time of Pope Benedict's visit to the United Kingdom gave a ratio of diocesan priests only (not religious) to people as 1:1,147. There is a pretty big difference between the situation in the United Kingdom and even our nearest neighbour! So, if the rest of the world is getting along with higher ratios, it would be foolish of us to imagine there is some greater crisis here than elsewhere. Of course, and this is common knowledge, in those areas of the world where the clergy are fewest, lay ministries are flourishing. It is a sign of the Spirit's activity we should not ignore!

We must agree that there is a chronic shortage of people to fill all those functions carried out by official agents of the Roman Catholic Church. This shortage, however, is not created by too few bishops, priests or deacons. It is created by unwillingness among some to let aspects of the Church's human organisation pass from clerical into lay hands. It has to make sense to let lay professionals do what they are better equipped to do than untrained clergy. This happens quite a lot at diocesan level but less so at parish level. However, the matter goes much deeper than this kind of co-responsibility. Tidying up human traditions to make church organisation more efficient is all well and good. In this book, however, we are considering matters not common to all human organisations but those specific to Christ's Church and what are they? They are the ways of serving and building up Christ's Church which the Spirit empowers all the baptised to carry out and how does he do this? He does it in the Sacraments of Christian Initiation and in the distribution of his free, charismatic, gifts. Immeasurably more serious than any reluctance on the clergy's part to give up administrative functions, is the development of ministerial roles in the Church's own life and mission that are simply a part of what it means to be baptised.

There have been enormous developments over the past 50 years and they are more advanced in some places than in others. Nevertheless it is appropriate to ask to what extent are people aware of the doctrinal basis for lay ministries? To what extent are they officially recognised in local churches as necessary expressions of the Church's life and mission? In some places, however generous the spirit in which tasks are undertaken, there are lay people and clergy who see the whole thing as nothing more than 'helping Father' to do his job. In what some people would see as more favourable circumstances (i.e. a proliferation of priests) these tasks would revert to those to whom they are thought properly to belong, the clergy. Such an attitude is a throw back to the official attitude to the lay apostolate before the Second World War - an attitude repudiated by the Second Vatican Council.

The situation the Church finds itself in, generally perceived as a shortage of clergy, is, in God's Providence, forcing the issue. Even so, we have to take seriously what the "Spirit is saying to the Churches" through the witness of the Second Vatican Council. It challenges Church policies and practices in every area of its life. This book does not look at all these challenges. It is confined to a reflection on the roles belonging to every member by reason of their Christian Vocation and Initiation. To recognise, to honour and to create a pastoral system which takes full account of what Christian Initiation has empowered all members to accomplish may be accelerated by a 'shortage of priests'. In itself, it is both a reform of bad practice and a development the Spirit is inspiring.

We must begin by taking seriously what Baptism and Confirmation empower all members of the Church to do. In addition, we have to recognise and honour the indispensable place of the Spirit's free or charismatic gifts. They are essential to the life and mission of the church, as the Second Vatican Council teaches.[3] With their recognition by the institutional church, a great flowering of ministries can be expected. Because I am a Roman Catholic, I gladly acknowledge the role of episcopal discernment in the exercise of these gifts in his local church. The charismatic and the institutional gifts complement each other. This does not alter the fact, however, that the bestowal of charismatic gifts does not fall under clerical control or patronage but is an exercise of the Sovereignty of the Spirit. The role of the institutional leaders is to discern, recognise and affirm when they judge the gifts to be genuine or, as the case may be, discern, refuse to recognise and forbid.

If the Third Millennium is to become an age of a New Evangelisation, Catholic Christians, indeed, any Christians brought up in faith communities where these considerations have been absent, need to carry out a prayerful, searching analysis of what they imagine being a Christian means. Why? Because the only kind of Christianity we can share with others is the kind we ourselves practice – you can't give what you don't have.

If we have grown up with a view of Christ's Church which focuses all attention on what the clergy do, or what the bishops do or what the Pope does, it is more than likely that we understand our place in it as little more than passengers. Worse, we may see going to church like a weekend call at a service station: customers supplied with the means of salvation by Church officials. There are historical reasons why so distorted a view of things could have dominated our upbringing as a Catholic. But this sad vision is not what the Church, attentive to the correctives in its doctrine and practice proclaimed in the Second Vatican Council, teaches nor celebrates in its worship.

Christians are people who, once ignorant of God's purpose, have come to believe that God has called them in Christ to his greatest gift. What is more, in granting them this gift, He asks them to share it with others. But what is this gift? We have to ask ourselves just how we envisage and appreciate it, for our particular vision of the Mystery of Faith is all we have to offer others.

What do we value most about Christ's Church; clarity of doctrine forcibly proclaimed? In this case we can sit back and let the bishops united with the Pope, or, as some might prefer, Vatican bureaucracy get on with running the church. Do we think the most important gift God's church can offer people of all cultures and languages are European liturgical traditions? Should a church that wishes to embark on a new evangelisation be concerned with preserving the inherited splendours of European music put at the service of a baroque misunderstanding of Liturgy, an ecclesiastical imitation of courtly ceremonial?[4] Let's don our birettas, lace albs and fiddle-back chasubles, leave church music to professional choirs and ignore all that Vatican II said about recovering an active participation of the whole people in the Sacred Liturgy.

Is Christianity a works and wages religion for us? Let's forget mission and earn as many indulgences as we can through our private devotions. Do we see ourselves only as God's creatures and servants of his law? Then let us put our nose to the grindstone and get on with it. Do we see the meaning of life as earning the reward of a servant's obedience? Then let's forget the grace of adoption offered us in Christ and get down to obeying the Law of Moses. None of us wants to embrace these perversions of the Holy Gospel but we must be even more direct in our questioning if we want to take our place in a new age of evangelisation.

Some people believe that human nature is so steeped in sin that the divine likeness has been irreparably damaged; that the only way to escape this damnation is to reach out with an explicit trusting faith in the Lord Jesus. If this is so, 99.9% of human beings who have ever lived, never had and never will have, the remotest possibility of actually hearing the Gospel that Jesus is Lord. They are excluded from God's purpose; damned. Is that what we have to offer? Is this to be the new evangelisation? Others take a less negative view, but fear that if the power of sin is not strongly emphasised the need for the cross – and there are those who do not mean Christ's cross but the need to put your own back into discipleship - will be down-played.

There are those, however, who proclaim their belief that God has a purpose for each and all human beings, attainable by all. The Church attests this faith, liturgically, at various times. The eighth of the solemn intercessions on Good Friday prays for those "who do not believe in God that they may find him by sincerely following all that is right".[5] God's purpose is a purpose of infinite love, beyond the human heart to conceive. The Church believes that in Jesus, crucified and risen, God has revealed and achieved His one plan and that He has established in this world a community of faith to be a sign of what He offers people of every tribe, language and nation. This sign is the universal or catholic community of faith we call Christ's Church. Its purpose is to share with others what it knows itself to have been given and is available to all. How is this gift revealed in Christ's Church?

In the fourth century, St. Monica prayed for her wayward son. Augustine. In infancy he had been dedicated but not baptised, a common enough practice then. He later took up various ways of life inconsistent with a Christian calling. Her one hope for him was, she said, "to see you become a Catholic Christian before I died".[6] In expressing her hopes in this way, she spoke, we must remember, from an experience of Christ's Church centuries before Orthodox and Latin Christians were divided and long before the upheavals of the sixteenth century divided Latin Christians into Catholics and Protestants. However, her aim for her son, to become a 'Catholic

Christian' suggests a comprehensive Christianity. It suggests a marriage between evangelical and sacramental visions of Christ's Church and holds in balance those distinct aspects of the Church we call the hierarchical and the charismatic or its structured and its free elements.

The Second Vatican Council, having pointed the way out of historical constraints on its vision and practice, calls all Christians to attain this harmonious balance in their vision of Christ's Church. Embracing this vision, the Roman Catholic Church of the twenty-first century believes itself called to and equipped for a new age of evangelisation. This restored vision is necessary for true evangelisation, for we can only give others what we already have. Proclaiming the Gospel of Christ is not the same thing as emphasis on particular doctrines to mark the differences between Protestants and Counter Reformation Roman Catholics at odds with each other. Proclaiming the Gospel is not the same thing as defending the role of 'Church', whether Catholic or Protestant in a social order that has gone with the wind. In short, proclaiming the Gospel cannot be identified with the kind of church some of us were brought up in. An era is over.

It was to free up the Church from this dead hand of history that the Second Vatican Council (1962-1965) was summoned by Pope John XXIII. Opening the Council, he shared with the Church an intuition which put into a visionary context the very purpose of the Council he believed himself inspired to summon. It is a vision that has always captivated me and which I believe all reform and renewal of the Church is meant to serve. The pope said, "Divine Providence is leading us to a new order of human relations which, by men's efforts, and even beyond their expectations, are directed towards the fulfilment of God's superior and inscrutable designs".[7] The challenge to rethink our understanding of all that has been handed down to us and which we are entrusted to hand on, demands a whole-hearted assent. We must make up our minds whether or not we believe that the grace of the Second Vatican Council was an experience of divine vocation to the whole Church or a mistaken human enterprise. I plump for the former.

It is itself a great challenge to examine the inherited priorities of post-Reformation and post-Enlightenment Roman Catholicism in the light of the Council's magnificent doctrine on the Mystery of Christ's Church, 'Lumen Gentium'. However, when we have espoused the more balanced understanding of the Church we find there, and remodelled its structures accordingly, there remains the question of who is to undertake the new evangelisation for the new age. This book is written in the conviction that nobody is called and nobody is empowered to share the life of the Church without being called to and empowered to share its mission. Whatever has to be said about the different roles proper to bishops, presbyters, deacons and lay ministers all questions are to be resolved within that context.

Those of us born into Catholic families and baptised as infants must re-examine the way we think about just what it is we have been called to and for what we have been empowered. How can we best do this? We were led to the sacrament of Baptism before we were capable of belief. We may reach a new awakening to all that we were led to by examining how adult believers, not yet permitted to approach Holy Baptism, are prepared to take this step. Our guide must be 'The Rite of Christian Initiation of Adults' (R.C.I.A.). This Liturgical document is a direct fruit of the Second Vatican Council and the Council's imperative decree that the Catechumenate must be restored. I well remember, as a parish priest, reading a study edition of this revolutionary document in the mid nineteen-seventies and thinking, "This is just wonderful, but the church to implement it does not exist".

I have always found that in matters Liturgical, the most profound truth is contained in what looks like detail. It may seem to some to be a mere ceremonial detail that R.C.I.A. couples Baptism and Confirmation. Not understanding the significance of this detail, there are those who ignore it. After all, in our upbringing we regarded their separation by many years as the norm. The rite that is to be observed in admitting adults to full life in the Church makes no doubt that Baptism and Confirmation are not to be separated. [8] Why is R.C.I.A. so emphatic on this point? As I understand it, these two sacraments are essentially linked – to this day, in the Eastern Rites (whether Orthodox or Uniate) infants are confirmed as soon as they are baptised. What is this all about?

I see Baptism as a sign of our vocation to discipleship and Confirmation as a sign of our vocation to apostleship. In both, we receive the Gift of the Holy Spirit empowering us to fulfil our calling. Without this Gift we have no power to live in Christ and are powerless to carry out the mission he has entrusted to his Church. Since they are not to be separated, something is being said which those of us baptised in infancy may need to hear. The Church does not deem adult believers to be ready for one without the other. A person is not ready for a full following of Jesus until that person is also ready to be sent. In other words, we cannot share the life of the Church without sharing its mission. This is the way the Church treats adult believers and those baptised in infancy must learn it too. There are no passengers in Christ's Church.

To become fully equipped for so great a calling, we have to be prepared. The Second Vatican Council's decision, that the Catechumenate must be restored was one of its most far-reaching. In ancient times, the Catechumenate was an indispensable stage in becoming a full member of the Church. The Council required its re-introduction into the mainstream of the Church's life because it did something that 'convert instructions' of recent times did not touch.

The Catechumenate was not for people who had not yet become believers. Only people who had already accepted the Gospel of Christ were admitted. Having said that, it guided them to embrace with a life-long commitment not only what it means to be a disciple but an apostle. Those of us who were baptised before we were believers must, somehow or another, claim the grace of our Christian Initiation by a deliberate, conscious, commitment to our vocation. By learning what kind of Christian formation the ancient Church offered believers before they were baptised, we can learn how we may be trained or formed. We all have to undergo Christian formation, whether this takes place before or after Christian Initiation. We all have to undergo a radical conversion that awakens us to the reality of our calling and the grace which empowers us to answer it.

God is good, and goodness, says St. Thomas Aquinas, is

"diffusivum sui"[9] or in plain English, goodness just has to spread itself around. In Jesus crucified and risen, the One God, Living and True has disclosed his eternal plan, his purpose for all mankind. Once we have come to realise something of the inestimable grace we have been called to, we shall want to do all that we can to share the joy it gives us with others. As the first letter of John says, "What we have seen and heard, we are telling you so that you too may be in union with us, as we are in union with the Father and with his Son Jesus Christ. We are writing this to you to make our own joy complete".[10] The joy that the faith gives us is the keynote. Joy is the sign of what Jesus described when speaking of the Spirit that was to be outpoured, he said, "The water that I shall give will turn into a spring inside him, welling up to eternal life",[11] and in another place, "Let the man who believes in me come and drink. From his breast shall flow fountains of living water".[12] When we have been touched by God's own goodness, we are bound to want to spread it around.

If there is to be a 'new evangelisation' in today's Church, its only source can be a recovery of this living fountain. We have in ourselves no power to evangelise. We cannot, in our own power, speak the Word of God that can move the mountains of indifference and ignorance about God. We cannot, in our own power, touch the innermost heart of another person with that Word which cuts more keenly than a two edged sword. We do not have the power within ourselves to expose a person to himself and produce the repentance that leads to life. We can, however, do such things in the power of the Spirit. That is why charismatic renewal, a rediscovery of the sovereignty of the Spirit in the life of the Church is utterly necessary if we are to become an evangelising church in this country. The ability to awaken faith in people who have not yet heard the Good News about Jesus Christ is exclusively the work of the Spirit. To form those who have become believers by handing on to them the riches of the Catholic tradition is the work of the Spirit. We have been entrusted with this holy word and we have to turn consciously to the Spirit within us, the source of the gifts we need if we are to be able to carry out the tasks entrusted to us. We must be utterly confident that what the Lord calls us to, he empowers us for. To be open to the power of the Spirit in whatever gifts he wishes us to have, is the only way to become an evangelist or catechist.

The challenge with which the Word of God confronts members of the Church today can be framed as a question each of us must ask ourselves, the question is this: has the ground work, the evangelisation in which real catechesis and real growth in the Christian way of life must be rooted, taken place in my own life? If I am to be a bringer of the Good News to others, this will be possible only if I myself am converted to the Good News. If I am to share with fellow believers the riches of the Church's doctrinal and sacramental tradition, I must know and love it. I cannot give what I have not got.

Now perhaps we can see that we can never become apostles if we have not become disciples. We can never be sent if we have not wholeheartedly assented to follow Jesus. We cannot be open to the gifts of the Spirit that will enable us be witnesses of the Good News except to the extent that we have assented to the cost of following Jesus into all that the Good News offers us.

This book offers reflections on how each of us may learn to

appreciate in a new way the gift the Lord calls us to receive, the gift he entrusts to us that others may share it. Knowing now what we have, we shall be able to give it.

Chapter One

My own experience of being called and sent

If you have picked up this book, the odds are that you are already trying to lead a Christian life; you are drawn to do so or you are at least interested in the idea. How each of us reached this point in our faith journey, with you enquiring and me wanting to share some thoughts about it with you, are probably very different stories. Even so, the more we seek to answer our calling, the more we find that deeper than the differences in our individual stories, there is but one mystery of God's grace. The mystery of grace operating in God's creation at large and revealed in Christ's Church is exactly the same grace at work in the depths of my heart and yours. It is the task of evangelists and catechists to enable us to realise this.

God never ceases to speak to human hearts whatever the obstacles that sin creates within us. "Even when man disobeyed you and lost your friendship you did not abandon him ...but helped all men to seek and find you."[1] In making this confession of faith of God's plan, the Eucharistic Prayer speaks of this mystery prior to any revelation made through Israel or Jesus Christ. The decision facing every person who comes into contact with the Christian Gospel is this: is the God, whom I have sought in the interior of my heart, inviting me to recognise him in the visible community of faith which proclaims the Good News of Jesus Christ?

In regard to this great mystery of grace, ever at work in God's creation, hidden from all human wisdom but now revealed in Christ, St. Augustine of Hippo speaks bold words. Reflecting on the relationship between the Word made flesh and each believer, he advises us to, "Keep before our eyes the very source of grace, taking its origin in Christ, our head, and flowing through all his members according to the capacity of each. The grace which makes any man a Christian, from the first moment of his coming to believe, is the same grace which made this man *(Jesus)* the Christ from *(the first moment of)* his coming to be man. The Spirit through whom men are reborn is the same Spirit through whom Christ was born. The Spirit by whom we receive the forgiveness of sins is the same Spirit who brought it about that Christ knew no sin."[2] The one story of mankind's relationship with God, described in all the stories that make up the Bible, is my story. It is your story. There is no other. When I begin to realise this, I am on the way to becoming a herald of the Good News of Jesus Christ.

We can know something about this mystery and appreciate aspects of it in a variety of ways. We have all had some kind of oral instruction whether through preachers, teachers, catechists, our parents or friends. Perhaps we have read books about doctrine, theology or spirituality. We have used different kinds of devotional exercises or prayer practices that appealed to our temperament and have helped us on our way. Like the lawyer who applauded the Lord's teaching on the greatest commandment, we perhaps share his joy in the truths he found there: "Well said, teacher. You are right...To love Him with all your heart, with all your understanding, with all your strength, and to love your neighbour as your self is worth more than all burnt offerings and sacrifices."

But having been brought thus far at God's calling, we may still need to hear the Lord's words, cutting as they do to our deepest hearts, "You are not far from the kingdom of God."[3]

I have often pondered what it might mean that so enthusiastic an answer to the Word of God still leaves us "not far" from the kingdom of God. In my own experience, it is as if over many decades, I have managed to hear the Lord say, "It is no good, Ambrose, the Word I speak cannot be squeezed into the way you see things. It challenges the very ground on which you stand before me." However, when the two edged sword of God's word does penetrate, there is an indisputable test of its authenticity. The test is this, bringing two realities into unity. The first is one's personal experience of the mystery. The second is this experience lived out within the community of faith. Here we have both an interior and exterior witness to the veracity of the Word addressed to us. The Spirit at work in both testifies to the truth in each. This is the harmony between the charismatic and institutional elements that make up the Church. This confirmation enables a Christian to fulfil his share in Christ's mission by speaking in Christ's name from the heart. In the words of Pope Paul VI, "In the long run, is there any other way of handing on the Gospel than by transmitting to another person one's personal experience of faith?[4] We share with others our faith in the one great truth of God's grace at work in all, by sharing our faith in its reality in our own lives.

POINTS OF DEPARTURE

In sharing with you ways I have perceived and, hopefully,

welcomed the coming of God into my life, I readily acknowledge that each one of us makes the journey of faith from different points of departure. A lady of my acquaintance is a profound Christian believer but not, like me, a Catholic Christian. We knew each other by meeting at celebrations of Charismatic Renewal. She shared with me her intense personal faith in Christ as her Lord and Saviour and how for some time she had been moving towards a recognition of His presence and activity in the Sacraments. From this she went on to realise the sacramental nature of the Church itself and even to acknowledge its basic visible structures, not its human traditions, as one of the Spirit's gifts. I spoke of how I had been aware of the visible structures of the Church from childhood and had been drawn to a great love of its sacramental nature. Through my sacramental union with Christ I had been moving, over the years, to a much more personal awareness of His presence as Lord in my life. Her uncomplicated reply shows the same grace working in different people, "Mine has been the same journey but in the opposite direction."

STARTING FROM WHERE WE ARE

I was born into a Catholic family who introduced me to Catholic religious practices, then sent me to Catholic schools where I was introduced to Catholic doctrine. During that experience, I wasn't aware that anyone wanted to convert me. It is almost as if those who brought me up and I myself had no idea that I had to be converted from anything. Wasn't I already in possession of what it took to be a Catholic Christian! As I reflected on this in later life, I realised that my childhood and youthful experience of the Christian way of life led me to make a number of false assumptions.

I assumed that to have a working knowledge of Catholic doctrine and morals was the same thing as having faith and, what is worse, that possessing such knowledge was the same thing as having heard and been converted to the Gospel of Jesus. Although I would not have been able to say so at the time, I am now able to say that it was only when I was in my forties, that I realised the basis of my religious life was not a heartfelt acceptance of God's grace in Jesus but some form of works and wages religion. I knew the words 'grace' and 'forgiveness', and had some faith in what I believed these words meant but I was definitely working my passage.

I want to stress that I have not the slightest doubt that the Living Lord was working on my conversion through the acquaintanceship with the Mystery of Faith given me in my childhood and adolescence and I am forever grateful to those through whom the Lord blessed me with it. However, there have been certain occasions, turning points in my life and my discipleship, when I was able to discern that I was clearly being spoken to and must choose how I would respond.

The first occurred on Good Friday, April 19th 1957
The second on Saturday, July 23rd 1978
The third on Saturday, 1st December 1990
And the fourth in the autumn of 1996

The first altered the course of my life forever because as a result of it I became a priest. The second altered the course of my life because it challenged me to take seriously my call to Christian discipleship in every aspect of my humanity. The third changed my perception of what I regarded as most important in Christ's Church. The last challenged me to be a witness in a way which others, especially some fellow clergy, who also loved and served Christ's Church, did not see as the work of God.

GOOD FRIDAY 1957

I was nineteen years old and coming to the end of my third year at a college of music and drama. I knew that when the course ended I should be required to complete two years of National Service in one of the armed forces. I had left school with no academic ambitions, desirous only of pursuing my dream of a career in the theatre. Before my experience on Good Friday, 1957, I had already been smitten by the mysterious beauty of the Easter Liturgy in 1955. A cousin and I had attended the Easter Vigil, restored that year after a millennium to its place on the night of Holy Saturday. Nearly sixty years on, both of us still talk about the wonder of the experience.

As an altar boy I had attended the Easter Vigil as it had been performed for a thousand years. I use the word 'performed' rather than 'celebrated' for that was exactly my experience as a boy in 1949. In a cold, early morning, the morning of Holy Saturday, the parish priest, some members of the parish choir and some altar boys went through a rigmarole which meant absolutely nothing to me or the handful of clergy and servers present. A 'fly in amber' is the image of the post-Tridentine Liturgy which springs to my mind, relics of a forgotten past, images that no longer had any meaning to the leadership in the church and which had long ceased to have any relevance to the general body of Catholics or their understanding of what it meant to be baptised. These memories of what life was really like as a worshipper in the Roman Catholic Church before liturgical reforms found their fullest expression in the Second Vatican Council, are enough to deter me from any sympathy with today's 'reform of the Liturgical reform'. I know and I remember what it was really like.

My experience of the restored Easter Vigil in 1955 was a moment of revelation. Although I did not have the language at the time to express what I now believe happened, I was gifted by that gift of the Spirit we called in days gone by, 'Fear of the Lord' or in more modern parlance, 'Awe in the presence of the Lord'. I had no idea what the Easter Vigil was saying to me. I only knew that I was awe-struck, a bit like Isaiah, I suppose, in his primary prophetic experience. What the liturgy was celebrating had nothing to do with what I had hitherto presumed Easter was all about. But, in my unknowing, I knew that being present, taking part in this act of worship, even though this was via a book, a missal in Latin with English translations of the texts, I was witnessing something that took me beyond any ideas I may have hitherto entertained about what it could mean to be a Catholic Christian.

I suppose that it was within the context of this earlier youthful experience that I attended the Good Friday liturgy in 1957. There, I heard the choir sing the Reproaches (sung in Vitoria's stunning polyphony). As I read in my Latin/English missal, "My people, what have I done to you? How have I offended you? Answer me" I broke down, for it seemed to me that the Lord was saying, "Ambrose, I just do not know what more I can do." I recall writing about that moment, "With my head buried in the fur collar of my camel-hair coat, I sobbed my heart out!" At that moment the Word of God which cuts finer than a two edged sword struck me where I was able to feel most deeply. That night I couldn't sleep. I knew that I was trying to ignore a living voice within, for fear of what might be the consequences if I listened. In the wee small hours, the words formed in my mind, "to be a priest". I was horrified. I wrestled with it for what seemed like hours and finally gave in. I made a choice, a choice I have never once been tempted to go back on or regret. As far as I was concerned, I caved in. I gave in to God and the choice to do so has determined the course of the rest of my life.

As I look back on it now, I am able to say that while I did surrender to the Lord, the depth of that surrender, which I thought was total, was actually not very deep at all. I realise now that this experience was a call to adult Christian discipleship. All these years later, I am able to say that within that renewal of my baptismal calling, I have been able to accept with joy any ministry to which the Church's leaders have called me. Being ready to accept a call from Church leaders to become a deacon and a presbyter was a fulfilling of that calling to adult faith and commitment. However, in order to get clear in our minds what the church is asking of us all today, there are some points to be cleared up about my understanding of vocation in those days for it may well linger on in others.

HAVING A VOCATION

Before the Second Vatican Council, the experience of being called to an adult Christian commitment, a sense of being called to serve the Church was bound to be experienced as a 'vocation to the priesthood or the religious life'. Indeed, one can go so far as to say, no popular preaching taught adult Christian Catholics to think of themselves as having a 'vocation'. My grammar school was run by Christian Brothers and I remember how they said marriage was a Christian vocation too but, even then, it seemed to me that this was such a patronising concession that I did not think they believed a word of it. A 'real' vocation was a special blessing given to priests and religious, monks, brothers or nuns – which they could lose if they were not careful!

Two other faulty theological strands were coupled with this narrow preaching about the meaning of vocation: the prevailing theology about the sacrament of Orders and an inherited vision of who, in the church, may properly be called 'apostles'. Both these subjects may seem very remote from an ordinary Catholic's understanding of their role in the Church. However, believe me; they are as important as the principles on which the combustion engine in your car works even though you may only want to know how to drive it! We have all been influenced by them and their influence cannot be realised if we are not conscious of them.

As to the prevailing theology about the sacrament of Orders, there was a respectable theological tradition going back to St. Jerome in the fourth century which questioned the very idea that the episcopate is a sacrament. He famously said, "What can a bishop do, apart from ordain, that a presbyter cannot do?"[5] You may well think that this opinion had something to do with the fact he had been secretary to successive popes without ever having been nominated bishop, I however cannot say. The Second

Vatican Council was to affirm that episcopacy most certainly is a sacrament and, moreover, it is the origin of both the presbyterate (commonly called 'the priesthood' in English speaking countries) and the diaconate.

Within the theology that prevailed before the Second Vatican Council, the presbyterate was seen as the essence of Holy Orders. The diaconate was understood as a stepping stone towards it and the episcopate, whether a sacrament or not, as the icing on the cake. When I became a seminarian this theology was expressly taught in a book published as late as 1962. "The principal meaning of the Sacrament of Orders is found in the presbyterate for which the diaconate is a preparation and episcopacy the final touch ('consumatio')."[6] Within a couple of years, the Second Vatican Council would turn this theology, almost literally, on its head. According to its teaching the episcopate is the fountain head of all the ordained ministry, presbyters and deacons being given distinct ways of sharing in that service to the community of faith.

During the Middle Ages, the idea of being called by God to serve the Church had become identified with being called to the 'clerical state.' Clerics were either lay men in minor orders or the sub-diaconate or men ordained to the diaconate, presbyterate or episcopate. This division between 'clergy' and 'laity' was a legal notion not a sacramental notion. Once a person was a cleric, he was in the service of the Church, no longer subject to civil laws but church laws. Some of the 'clergy' who were, in fact, cardinals of the Roman Church, were laymen in minor orders. Once the idea that there was a 'division of labour' where clerics governed the 'spiritual' and non-clerics the 'temporal', it was inevitable that there grew up a vision of the Church that only the successors of The Twelve and the clergy associated with them could be spoken of as having an apostolic ministry. This was a confusion of different roles.

It is one thing to be responsible in the Church for discerning and giving authentic teaching on what is and what is not Catholic Faith; this is the distinctive ministry of bishops. It is quite another, "Always to be ready to give an explanation to anyone who asks you for a reason for your hope."[7] This is nothing less than the privileged responsibility of every member of the Church, anointed in their Christian Initiation as 'priest, prophet and king' and entrusted with Christ's good name. Not all apostles were numbered among the Twelve, notably, St. Paul, not to mention the lady Junia, described as "prominent among the apostles".[8] All bishops are sent but not all who are sent are bishops.

GOOD ORDER IN THE CHURCH

Anyone wishing to exercise any form of ministry must do so in communion with the local church's bishop. Indeed, my entire understanding of ministry would fall apart without this ecclesial dimension. However, that is an entirely different thing from identifying Divine vocation with Ecclesial vocation. To illustrate the foolishness of conflating the two it suffices to point out that when I was nineteen years old, it was culturally impossible for me to tell my bishop that God was calling me to be a deacon. Half a century later, men can now do this and, in addition, men can still volunteer for priestly ordination in the belief that God is calling them to be priests. However, I still cannot knock on my bishop's door to announce that God is calling me be to be a bishop.

This last statement sounds so silly to our ears because, whatever the faults in the current Roman Catholic system by which heirs to the college of bishops are chosen, the paradox is that choosing remains an essentially ecclesiastical matter. Nobody can volunteer to become a bishop because they think God is calling them to this office. The process of choosing baptised Christians to become bishops begins and ends with people who exercise apostolic leadership advising others that in the Church's judgment one is called to the ordained ministry. This is the only valid meaning of having a 'vocation' to the episcopate, presbyterate or diaconate. One has a vocation to the ordained ministry by being called, by existing church leaders, to the ordained ministry! The extent to which the Holy Spirit is involved in an ecclesial vocation is, of course, a separate question. The short answer is that to the extent that the Spirit is invited into the process, He will surely be present. However, it does seem rather preposterous to blame the Holy Spirit for all the mistakes bishops have made in their exercise of discernment in this matter!

Divine vocation is a call to a whole-hearted following of Christ and a whole-hearted sharing in the church's mission. Within that context of divine grace, it is the responsibility of Church leaders to discern the suitability of individuals to a ministry requiring sacramental ordination. We have laboured too long in the Latin Church with the mistaken notion that God calls only young, celibate men to be sharers in the ordained ministry. It is the visible authority in the Church which calls only young, celibate men to the presbyterate and subsequently to the episcopate. What God thinks about this ecclesiastical policy is something upon which there is some division in the Church.

To appreciate the theme of this book, that every person admitted to Christian Initiation is both called to be a disciple and sent to be an apostle, we must face the fact that within the historical development of the ordained ministry in the Roman Catholic Church, the *canonical* mission given to ordained ministers has, for many people, become identified with the meaning of the Sacrament of Orders. Because Canon Law permits only the clergy to carry out certain functions, these are assumed to be 'priestly' or 'diaconal' of their nature. Common sense, however, tells us that the office of parish priest is an amalgam of functions, for most of which, it would be ludicrous to imagine one needed a sacramental initiation of any kind, let alone ordination. I have never forgotten reading something that Sir Anthony Kenny wrote about his experience as a curate in 1950's Liverpool. It dawned on him that to fulfil the greater part of what was expected of him as a Catholic priest in the ecclesiastical set-up of the time, he did not need to believe a thing about Christianity, much less about Catholicism and its priesthood. He realised that he didn't believe any of it and so left it all behind to become a distinguished, agnostic, academic.[9]

Although at nineteen years of age, I simply said, "Yes" to the idea of giving my life to God, - concretised in the idea that this meant becoming a priest – I did learn early on what I came to regard as the essential difference between the divine call to adult commitment and the ecclesial call to the ordained ministry. The only priests I had ever known in my parish life were Benedictines, and so, after National Service, I was a postulant at Belmont Abbey in Herefordshire. I have always valued my experience there, not least because it gave me a full year's experience of the pre-Vatican II liturgy in all its unreformed state, something that has always enabled me to value the correctives of the Tridentine Rite which the Second Vatican Council authorised. But, more personally, it enabled me to discern the difference between the ministries of the ordained and the non-ordained. I could see the value of a rule of life in Christian discipleship and the value of belonging to a community engaged in the Church's mission. However, neither of these seemed to me directly to do with the service of leadership and it was to be a leader that I believed I was being drawn.

Ordained in 1966 I was shortly after asked to be my Archbishop's secretary and remained so until becoming a parish priest in 1974. My assessment of the period between my ordination and 1978 is that I took over my vocation. I have no recollection of Archbishop Murphy actually telling me off but I do remember his mentioning the advice given to him by Bishop Moriarty, Bishop of Shrewsbury, when he himself was his co-adujutor bishop: "Take your hands off the handle-bars!" Whatever may be said about any inappropriate actions on my part in regard to running the diocese, I gladly confess that in my personal, spiritual life, my hands were firmly on the handle bars.

SATURDAY, JULY 23rd 1979

During the first decade of my life as a priest, I was happy to accept, by and large, the theological, moral and spiritual formation I had been given in the seminary and acquired by my own interest and studies. All this formed a secure framework in which I happily lived and worked as a diocesan priest. Everything I understood about my calling fitted into my way of seeing things. However, in a journal which I started keeping in mid 1975 I began to record serious misgivings about the way ahead. Many entries show that I had no idea of what it was that disturbed me but they also declare my readiness, so I protested to the Lord, to face whatever had to be faced in order to move on from the dead-end I found myself in. The last of these was written during a holiday visit to my old seminary in Spain and I believe does authentically express a readiness to face the unknown.

At Viana de Cega, the country house of the English College, Valladolid, I wrote, on 17th July, 1979, "With all the honesty I can speak with, I ask the Lord to draw me into the crucifying consciousness of his redeeming love. With whatever consciousness I have of my unfaithfulness, weakness, self interest and wilfulness, I beg to approach ever nearer to the holiness of His divine love. To back off from God because of our sense of unholiness is a flight from reality. We must gladly suffer the experience of our unholiness in the presence of Him whose love re-creates and makes us holy with his own holiness. If there lie before me nothing but years of embarrassment and horror at my self-centredness before my loving Lord, I beg to dive into it, rather than stand back. It is you alone Lord whom I seek, enable me to face the appallingness of my unworthiness to be with you. Only by coming to you through this bitter valley shall I come to your dwelling place. I beg not to shirk the task, not to waver from the path along which you are calling me. You are close to me a sinner; you are with me. Enable me to come close to you by recognising the greatness of your love for one, so unholy without you." Was this prayer answered?

The day after my return to my parish, the bottom fell out of my world. I was plunged into a turmoil of emotions, uncertainties and fears. I came to know misery and suffering such as I had never before experienced. This excruciating pain went on for a whole year. Indeed, it carried on into further years of refocusing my entire perception of what it must mean to believe that the Lord is at the centre of one's life, calling one to the centre of who one actually is, to live in His truth of who you actually are. What caused all this? I fell in love.

This was not for the first time in my life by any means, but it was the first time when I knew I was being touched in the deepest recesses of my heart. However bewildering, however destructive of my self-made world it was, and unable to bring to God anything but my need, I knew I was living in the truth, raw though it be. Even as everything I thought I knew about what it means to be a human being, about being a Christian, about being a priest collapsed, even as I was panic-stricken and cried, "How can God be in this?" there was, at a deeper level, perhaps not a peace, but a certainty that the Lord was saying, "You asked for the way ahead and this is it. There is no way round; the way is straight through the middle." I did indeed surrender to God's calling and guidance at a much greater level than hitherto. It was at this stage of my life that I learned a truth that has guided me ever since. I had become familiar with Aelred Squire's book 'Asking the Fathers' during the 1970s but had set it aside. On re-reading its opening chapters, I read that "The only security *(which authentic Christian tradition about the spiritual life offers)* is that of always being ready to pass beyond what one imagined one understood."[10] I was to spend the next six years re-reading the first six chapters.

This mid-life crisis required me to face, head on, instincts and emotions that had been foolishly ignored for decades and it was, naturally, in their unattended, immature, adolescent reality that they emerged and had to be integrated into my conscious life. It meant re-examining assumptions about the nature of things picked up from dubious philosophies and theologies – all passing as the Word of God in my assumptions. Once in a moment of prayer when my wounds seemed like an excruciatingly tender boil, it seemed to me that I experienced the hand of God extended in a soothing gesture and I cried out in fury, "Take your hand away!" recoiling from His touch. Another time, when I was more at ease, it was as if I heard the words, "Ambrose, gather the fragments" and I burst into tears knowing that without respect for what actually is, independently of the way I see things, I had clumped through God's creation as if it were a world of my own creation – which, of course, it had been.

This experience of visiting psychic and spiritual wounds, of looking for and finding healing at different levels continued from 1979 for nearly a decade until, as I well remember, a lady of deep spiritual perception whom I had known since the middle seventies, whose affection and wise counsel I cherished, said to me, "Father, you look so well." And I replied, "Thank you, Nora. I know deep within myself that I am well."

SATURDAY, DECEMBER 1st 1990

In 1990, my life as a Catholic and priest took a new turning. As one wit among my fellow clergy put it, "The world is turning upside down: they are freeing Nelson Mandela and Ambrose Walsh has been seen at a meeting of Charismatics." I had, hitherto been seen as a rather faithful servant of ecclesiastical institutions. Coupled with this, I had a deep reverence for the sacramental reality of Christ's Church, described by Pope Paul VI, in words that had thrilled me in 1964, "I believe the Church is a Sacrament, a Mystery, that is to say, a concrete reality penetrated by the Divine Presence."[11] As I have already mentioned, I had first been overwhelmed by the Divine Presence penetrating the concrete reality, when I attended the Easter Vigil in 1955. With this way of looking at the church, I really couldn't see the point of Charismatic Renewal. In this I was wrong and had to be led to an appreciation of the balance which should exist between the hierarchical or institutional gifts of the Spirit and the charismatic gifts of the Spirit. Above all I had to learn of the sovereignty of the Spirit in Christ's Church.

A person very close to me was sick with a brain tumour which was to cause his death in 1991. During the last year of his life, he came into contact with Charismatic Renewal and was very keen to share with me what he had experienced. Thus it was that I was called, kicking and screaming into a dimension of the Church's mystery that as yet I had no awareness of or, to the extent that I was aware, I had no inclination to know more about.

I can never be grateful enough for the grace that led me into an appreciation of the charismatic gifts of the Spirit and the absolute need for them in the mission of the Church. The first occasion on which I allowed myself to be prayed with by fellow believers was December 1st 1990. When asked what I wanted to be prayed for I made a general acknowledgement of my need for God's guidance, carefully saying nothing out loud about what I knew to be the real obstacles to a total opening up to the sovereignty of the Spirit. Someone whose name I do not know even to this day, spoke a word that cut more finely than any two-edged sword, reaching into a trauma I had experienced when I was three years old, speaking with a loving knowledge of who I am and offering healing. "Why do you doubt my love for you? I go before you with a father's love and my gift to you is wisdom." I knew then that the game was up. I could no longer hide from the immanence of the One who had always been calling me to live in the truth that would set me free.

I gradually came to see the importance of Charismatic Renewal in the context of the Spirit's call to a renewal of the whole Church, in all its aspects, in the Second Vatican Council. This realisation, dawning upon me in my personal experience of God's grace was confirmed in the words, the astonishing words of Pope John Paul II, "The Holy Spirit radically changes people and history. This was the experience of the Second Vatican Council, when the Church *rediscovered* the charismatic dimension as *essential to her identity.*" [12]

I had long been converted to the idea that the Liturgical movement, bearing fruit in the reforms authorised by the Second Vatican Council, revealed that the Church had lost consciousness of the meaning and value of something at the heart of its life. Now I came to realise that the sovereignty of the Spirit, his utter freedom of action, was also something essential to the Church's proper identity, and was, like liturgical worship, an essential feature of its existence which the modern Church would have to rediscover if it was to become what the Lord was calling it to be. What happens at the broadest level happens at the most intimate, personal level. If the Spirit was calling the whole Church to a new awakening, that is exactly what had to happen in me. It had happened to me in regard to the Church's sacramental dimension way back in 1955. Now it had to take place in regard to the Charismatic dimension of the Church and my personal sharing in its life and mission. .

AUTUMN 1996

In each of these turning points in my life I believed the hand of God to have been in them. That I believe this to be the case is no reason for anyone else to believe it. However, the test of authenticity I mentioned at the beginning this chapter is the only one to be applied. The authenticity of one's personal experience of the mystery is tested by one's life and mission within the community of faith. I can only say what I believe the Lord has done in my life; what fruit this belief has brought to the community of faith I serve must be left for others to judge. This has to be especially true of the fourth life-changing events of autumn, 1996. I did something that I knew would seem to others to take me beyond what it means to be a faithful priest. I however, believed I was being called to duty. I was being challenged by the Lord to act not only as an adult Christian but, more particularly, as someone ordained to be a fellow worker with my bishop for the well-being of our local church.

Indeed, within this responsibility, grave in itself, I had moreover, accepted the role of canon and a member of the diocesan College of Consultors. In short, I had to do precisely what I had always believed the word 'presbyter' meant: exercise co-responsibility for leadership of my local church.

During the course of my priestly ministry I have been called upon to fulfil various responsibilities in my local church apart from being a parish priest and in 1985 I was appointed a Diocesan Consultor. In the autumn of 1996 I found myself having to give very serious thought to my position. The external circumstances which occasioned this crisis, however grave they may have been, are not the issue here. This is about how a person judges life's situations in the light of the belief that God calls and sends us.

Suffice to say that in exercising my consultative role I became quite isolated, holding views not shared by others and so resigned my position in 1998. When this became public knowledge two years later, a brother priest took me to task for airing what he called my "personal disagreement" with Church authorities. I replied that were his analysis correct, I should have to accept his reprimand. However, I added, not flippantly, I hope, that what he had said was like telling me that the prophet Amos had a difference of opinion with the temple authorities of Samaria. I had acted on what I saw, rightly or wrongly, as the exercise of my responsibility as a presbyter and for this I should have to answer to the Lord.

Being called by God may seem to us in its beginnings as one aspect of our life among others. This, however, cannot be the case. Following our call will lead us on an inner journey and an outer journey. This life-long journey in faith will reveal who we are, why we are and how we are to become all that we were created to be. We have to come one way or the other, swiftly or slowly, to accept or reject that being called and sent by the Lord is the central, defining reality in our lives.

THE LAST ACT

Given leave to retire from parish work in 2000, I have spent the last eleven, very happy years, giving talks and fulfilling weekend supplies in parishes. It has also, at long last, given me the time to write these lines. I do so in the hope that I can share with a wider circle what I have preached in parishes and tried to effect in pastoral programmes.

When in 1957 I first assented to the idea of becoming a priest in the Roman Catholic Church, more than a few features of its life in those days did not appeal to me. Nevertheless, I assented to serving the institution as I knew it. Within a year, Pope John XXIII announced that he would call an Ecumenical Council and it was not until 1963 that I even began to realise what a life-changing event it was to be for all the Church. I cannot say when it first dawned on me but at some time after I began working as a diocesan priest, I realised that within God's providence I had never been called to serve the model of Church that had prevailed during my childhood and adolescence. On the contrary, I had been called to become a servant of the reform and renewal that the Second Vatican Council was to proclaim.

It was in obedience to the Council as the supreme expression of the Church's teaching authority that I took up and exercised the pastoral ministry. The kind of Church I tried to create in parishes I served was modelled not on the 1917 Code of Canon Law and its assumptions about apostolic mission and the relationship between clergy and laity but on the Second Vatican Council's corrective doctrinal insights. What that has meant to me we may now explore.

Chapter Two

Come, follow me

The word 'disciple' means 'follower' and 'apostle' means 'one sent'. Both words, therefore, express movement but in opposite directions. The first suggests motion inwards, to Jesus, who brings us to the Father's heart. The second moves outwards to those still ignorant of God's gift. Later on, we may give our attention to what it means to be sent. However, it is impossible to do that without first reflecting on what it means to have been called, who it is who calls and what it is we are called to. God, in Christ is calling us and Christ calls us to follow him into the Paschal Mystery and thus to the bosom of the Father.

To contemplate our being called by God to follow Jesus, we may begin by reflecting on the Gospel according to John's description of Jesus' first action and words. His first action is to turn. Two disciples of John the Baptist, in obedience to the prophet, are trailing after him. Jesus responds to their interest in him. ("Seek and you shall find.")[1] In this moment we may see how in the providence of God, for every one who will find faith in Jesus Christ, there is a time of honest search before the hidden God reveals himself. We do not know whom our heart seeks. "What are you looking for?" says Jesus to them. This hidden God has been bringing us to this moment and when we respond to the concrete experience in which he addresses us, even though we still do not know who it really is who calls us and to what we are called, the way is open. "Rabbi, where are you staying?" In response to their seeking, they hear those most gracious words, "Come and you will see."

Perhaps because I remember the day and the hour when I first set out on an adult following of Jesus, I am deeply moved by these words from the first chapter of the Gospel according to John which recall the day and the hour that Andrew and the beloved disciple first met Jesus. It is commonly agreed that the Gospel according to John was written towards the end of the first century, that is to say, seventy years after the death of Jesus. Yet, even after so many decades, the writer can look back and recall the time and place his life was to change for ever. I see the eyes of an old man filled with tears of gratitude as he shares with his disciples the memory of that moment: "it was about four in the afternoon."[2] An unforgettable moment of grace.

We can see what it means to believe that the living God is calling one in the concrete events of our every day life in the action of Philip, called by Jesus the day after Andrew and the man who was to become Jesus' beloved disciple had spent their memorable hours with him.

NATHANAEL

Philip wanted his friend Nathanael to share what he had experienced and introduced him to Jesus. At the first moment of their encounter Jesus called him "a true Israelite" and in a play on the name 'Israel', which means 'crafty' or 'deceitful', said that he knew Nathanael to be a man without guile. Asked how he knew this, Jesus said, "I saw you sitting under the fig tree." We come to this scripture understandably ignorant of colloquial turns of phrase common in Palestine two thousand years ago but we also come already believing that Jesus is God. In these circumstances we might presume that the God-man is simply claiming an ability to see beyond the ordinary range of human vision: that he actually saw the man sitting under a fig tree and that this simple fact should be enough for Nathanael to recognise him as more than human. You may believe that this is all the Gospel writer is saying.

However, you may wish to know that in the world of Nathanael and Jesus, "sitting under the fig tree" was a colloquial expression taken from the practice of seeking a very shady, peaceful spot where one could mediate on Holy Scripture. In effect, when the stranger from Nazareth summed up his personality in the most complimentary terms as "a true Israelite", Nathanael, with some surprise, asks, "How do you know *me*?" Jesus gives the breath-taking reply, "Nathanael, *I* have always known you when you are at your prayer." Jesus, or, as we may say with John, the eternal Word of God made flesh, is saying to Nathanael that at the most intimate moments of Nathanael's prayerful heart-searching before God, "I know you." They suggest a joy in God that a human being is actually seeking him, or more truly, that a human being is responding to the attraction God offers. A love deeper than the seeker can imagine longs for the one who seeks him to know him as he really is. This is what is going on when any one seeks God.

Recall the Lord's words to others he judges not so open to the reality of what is happening in their experience: "The Father who sent me has testified on my behalf. But you have never heard his voice nor seen his form. You search the scriptures because you think you have eternal life through them: even they testify on my behalf. But you do not want to come to me to have life."[3] In the light of these words, what does the Gospel writer suggest in putting on the lips of Jesus testimony that he saw Nathanael sitting under the fig tree?

In his greeting, Jesus speaks to Nathanael as the God of Israel whom Nathanael sought in his scripture-rooted prayer He challenged him to bring together two realities: his authentic search for God and God's answer to his prayer in offering him, through Philip, an invitation to meet Jesus. Secondly, in order that this may be so, he invited Nathanael to go beyond his ignorant but honest assumptions about God and be challenged by the fact that the God he seeks is actually answering him from what he thinks impossible: "Can anything good come from Nazareth?" God from God-forsaken Nazareth?

It dawns on Nathanael that what he has been seeking in his prayer is now being offered him in the flesh, and he calls Jesus, "Rabbi", "Son of God" and "King of Israel". Jesus answers, once again drawing on the biblical traditions about the Patriarch Jacob. Sleeping one night at an ancient shrine Jacob saw in his dream a staircase uniting heaven and earth with God's messengers going up and down and called the place where he had laid his head, Bethel: house of God. Jesus speaks of *himself* as this very point where the eternal and the temporal meet, the meeting place of heaven and earth. "Do you believe because I told you that I saw you under the fig tree? You will see greater things than this. You will see the sky opened and the angels of God ascending and descending on the Son of Man."[4] As Nathanael reflected on the words now spoken to him, what must he have felt when he recalled the next words spoken to Jacob; "I am the Lord… Know that I am with you. I will protect you wherever you go... I will never leave you until I have done what I promised you."[5]

FINDING GOD IN THE CONCRETE

We see in this exchange how the Good News of Jesus confronts us with the enormous challenge of living by faith: can it be that the God I have been seeking within my heart, or indeed, consciously avoiding there, invites me to recognise his real presence in my life in the human being, Jesus? During the days of his mortality, this meant recognising the meeting between God and mankind in the person of Jesus of Nazareth. Now that this man, crucified and risen is established as the Glorified Christ, it means recognising him in the concrete reality of the Gospel-rooted community of faith, his Church, the Body of Christ on earth. Nathanael took a step in this faith: all that his heart had led him to search for in the interior world of his prayer was actually being offered him in the concrete circumstances of his life on earth. The step he took in faith was taken not into the realms of some mythical fantasy but into the flesh and blood realities of daily life and he believed that God's providence had brought him to this moment of choice.

THE CHOICE TO HEED JESUS' CALL

Whatever way the Lord's call comes to us, the providence of God has in some way prepared us for it, however radically the call may challenge what we think we already know. The people who became Jesus' first disciples already had faith in the God of Israel before they ever knew Jesus. Indeed, their response to Jesus' call was made precisely as an expression of this faith. In following Jesus as a prophet sent by God, they brought all the ideas and expectations that this background had given them. They took a step believing they knew what they were doing and had an idea where they were going. The Gospel, however, testifies that they repeatedly failed to understand what Jesus was saying. They came to Jesus with ideas of what the Reign of God might mean, that is why they followed him. What they did not know is that these ideas, although they had set their feet on the right path, would turn out to be totally inadequate and would have to be given up before they would ever be able to enter the kingdom. I well recall sitting in the Easter Vigil at a time of great darkness in my life a period of what I thought was a time of failure and hearing, as for the first time in my life, God's holy Word,

"My ways are not your ways my thoughts are not your thoughts... The word that goes from my mouth does not return to me empty without carrying out my will and succeeding in what it was sent to do."[6]

Our call to be ever ready to move forward into the unknown may seem too daunting, so there is something we must remember. The most inadequate notions of what is right and good, the most meagre notions of what God is like, the merest breath of generosity of heart, all these things are already the result of God's grace at work in us. He it is who first set our feet on this path. It takes only what we might judge to be a little thing for God to slip through the crust of our selfishness and ignorance. It is simply that if we are going to let him reign, we must allow him, in the words of the psalm, to "burst the gates of bronze and shatter the iron bars"[7] of the imprisoning limitations in which ignorance and sin entrap us. I sometimes think that God will win no greater victory in us than that first moment of grace when we permit the reality of being called by Him to touch us.

Those who followed Jesus of Nazareth came to believe that God was sending them to the whole world with Good News that Jesus is Lord, but they did not take God's Word as they had understood it when they first came to Jesus. Yes, they came initially to Jesus, in the hope that he was 'the one to come'; they looked forward to Jesus ushering in the Reign of God. And yes, these same people later preached that in Jesus, crucified and risen, God had established his Kingdom. But between their initial following and their being sent, a revolution had taken place within them.

This revolution was not simply a matter of learning new ideas. If the journey of faith was to lead them out of their ignorance of God it had to take them through the depths of their ignorance about themselves. They had to learn by experience, the denuding truth that there is nothing in us, nothing in our sinful, mortal nature that is capable of bringing about the Reign of God. It is all gift. They had brought to Jesus of Nazareth some kind of faith but they had to learn by experience their radical inability to keep faith with him.

They had to pass through the depths of their radical need for God's forgiveness and healing if their hearts were to be open to all that God longed to share with them: his own Holy Spirit. He who went before them on this journey said, "The truth will set you free".[8] In dying, Jesus laid down his sinless life, humanly incapable of bringing about the Reign of God. He submitted, sinless though he was, to the limitations of being human. He yielded totally to the power of God to save mankind for no other reason than his love in our regard. His human being, his human heart became, in being raised up from the impotence of death, the source of eternal life, life in the Spirit.

Can you see how even as the Lord Jesus was undergoing the Paschal Mystery, those who were to find life through its power and be his heralds had to lose, so it seemed, everything that was merely human in their discipleship if they were ever to receive what had really been offered them in their initial calling? They were to discover that nothing was lost; it was transfigured beyond their imagining. I see this truth revealed in the experiences of those called to be witnesses of the Resurrection, in particular Thomas and Mary Magdalene.

THOMAS

The very structure of the fourth Gospel reveals that the climax and purpose of the book is that we should come to the same faith which enabled Thomas to recognise in the crucified and risen Jesus, "My Lord and my God."[9] My profound respect for this great witness to Jesus, dismissed by some as 'doubting Thomas' is based on the way the Gospel writer introduces him to us. As the gospel narrative unfolds, and it becomes ever clearer to the disciples that Jesus of Nazareth is not turning out to be what they thought he would be, as the disappointment mounts and they realise that they answered a call that has led them to nothing of what they had expected, when it is clear that the game is up and that Jesus, going to Jerusalem, is heading for disaster and death, what is Thomas's response? "Let us go and die with him."[10]

These words speak to me of such anguish, such lost hopes. It is a negative, pessimistic version of those words the same gospel puts on the lips of Peter, "to whom shall we go?" Thomas strikes me as somebody who feels doomed by love. Not that he regretted his love or believed he had been seduced; it is simply that he has been caught up in a tragic, hopeless love. To this extent, he is living in the truth. Although he cannot see it, God is calling him, in and through the very experience of loss of all that he thinks is possible in his love for Jesus, to something infinitely beyond the power of his mind and heart to conceive. He is right that according to all human judgement, only death is the end.

It is this broken heart, it seems to me that is shocked and offended by what he judges to be the inability of the others to face up to the brutal truth, the reality of the loss. He sees them, as we would say today, living in denial. The Paschal Mystery has brought him face to face with how life was meaningless without the one who alone had come to give it meaning. It is only when he has been brought to this point that he is able to receive the totally free gift of God's liberating truth. Only when he has reached this depth of emptiness is he able to recognise the utterly un-hoped for, unexpected vibrant presence of the one he had thought he already knew, "My Lord and my God."

Does not the Gospel writer say that it is precisely so that we too may come to this point that he has written his book? "Jesus did many other signs in the presence of his disciples that are not written in this book. But these are written that you may come to believe that Jesus is the Messiah, the Son of God and that through this belief you may have life in his name."[11]

THE APOSTLE TO THE APOSTLES

I have often asked myself why it was that Mary Magdalene was the first to be blessed with the gift of Easter faith. I like to think I was given a hint by the image of this weeping woman, stooping to look into the darkness of what she already knew as a totally empty tomb. Jesus was not only dead, he was now gone forever, beyond her touch. His disappearance robbed her even of some gesture of love and respect for his dead body. We all know what it is like when we have lost something important to us. We hunt in the same places over and over, hoping against hope that we are in the wrong and it is not lost forever. Why did Mary not give up, even when she already knew that the Jesus was dead and gone?

It seems to me that without knowing it she had already come to Easter faith even though what she staked all her hope on was beyond her power to imagine. Here was someone of whom it was said that Jesus had freed from 'seven devils', somebody who had known by experience the bonds of sin, the hopelessness of our entanglement with all that is not of God. But, through the graciousness of this man Jesus, she knew she had been freed and only God can forgive sin. She knew that God was in what she had experienced at the hand of Jesus. If he was now swallowed up in death, if God was not with him then her freedom from sin was illusory. She was back in her trap. In the darkness she knew that God was with her through the forgiveness and liberty in which she stood before God. And so, even if the possibility of Jesus' having been raised from the power of death had not entered her imagination, she could not deny what she knew in her heart: she had been raised up to God by him. She was already living in the faith that through Jesus she was reconciled to God. She had already accepted from God, at the hand of Jesus, the deeply personal gift of being made free of sin. In this faith, she heard her name spoken by the only one who really knew her and was the abiding source of her communion with God. "Mary!" "Rabounni!"[12]

CALLED TO RECEIVE AND SENT TO GIVE

Mary was sent to tell the Twelve that Jesus was alive and he would meet them. How do you imagine they received this news? The last time he saw them they were fleeing for their lives rather than be associated with him. How would you feel if some friend whom you had abandoned when being mugged, asked you to call into the hospital to see him? They must have been terrified of what he would say, expecting a just judgement on their infidelity. The very least that would be expected would be an explanation and an apology.

I see in this small group of people in Jerusalem around 30 AD, called by Jesus but utterly unfaithful to him, the entire human race, the children of Adam, standing before the judgement of almighty God. This group are bound to have known and accepted the justice of the judgement that should be passed on them. This is not the Good News but the point to which we must be brought if we are to actually hear it, believe it, and believing what is happening to us, accept the free gift.

What God's judgement, brought to us by the risen Lord Jesus turns out to be, goes beyond anything that the mind or heart can conceive. The first fruit of sin was that darkness of mind that makes us so ignorant of God's love that we flee into the bushes at the sound of his voice. To heal in us this root of sin, Jesus stood in the midst of those that had abandoned him and pronounced God's judgement on every insult and injury we are responsible for throwing at him: "Peace be with you." The Sacred Liturgy of Good Friday, designed to lead us into this great mystery, may well reproach us, but only that we may come to this point of repentance and hear the truth that sets us free.

Who can believe such goodness? Can it be that this moment is the end of our quest? Is this heart-stopping expression of unfailing love for sinful mankind the goal of our calling: to recognise and accept the forgiveness Christ offers? No.

More amazing yet, he breathes into us the very life by which he now lives saying, "Receive the Holy Spirit". Not only are we lifted out of the dead end in which sin would leave us, he transforms us in our innermost being, sharing with us the life he now lives with the Father. Do these wonders never cease? What more is possible?

If the wonders of God's grace, revealed in these brief words, do not utterly dumbfound us, the most astonishing is yet to come. The healing we have received, the grace in which we stand, this mighty work of God does not end there. "As the Father sent me, so I am sending you."[13] He who has revealed to us the Father's care for all mankind sends us, yes even us, to others with the gift we have received. He has entrusted to us the honour of his Holy Name. We are freed, raised up and sent.

In a later chapter we shall ponder on what it means to have been sent by the Lord, entrusted with the honour of his holy name. But first of all we have to face up to the fact that we can give only what we already have and that if we are to be able to give, we have first to receive for we are not the authors of what we hand on. It is nothing less than God's Gift. That we may receive God's Gift we must experience our need for the Gift if our humanity is to be fully restored to God's image and likeness and docile to his guidance. Called to follow Christ, we are called to face sin if we are to face grace. We must discover his guiding hand in everything we judge to be loss, diminishment and darkness no less than in those things we more easily imagine we discern as graces. We have to come face to face with that astonishing mystery of sin and grace which the Easter Proclamation speaks of in words so bold they are beyond our understanding,

> "O happy fault, O necessary sin of Adam
> which gained for us so great a Redeemer!"[14]

He who has called us in Jesus Christ has, as we say nowadays, 'faced down' sin and death. In the weakness of our humanity and in the power of the Spirit, he has led the way for us into the Paschal Mystery, and has said, "I am the way, the truth and the life. No one comes to the Father except through me."[15]

The people Jesus called thought they had some idea of what they were being invited into and that is why they followed. The same happened to us. But their following took them on a journey they had never made before. The characteristic feature of this journey is a paradox, a turning upside down of all that our human judgement calls wisdom. The journey leads into the depths as the only way of reaching the heights. It enters the darkness as the only way of reaching the light. It leads us into the loss of everything in order to gain all. The journey is called 'The Paschal Mystery'. It is the journey Jesus made in his dying and rising and before making it he said to others, "Come, follow me." Through the Sacraments of Christian Initiation we are incorporated into this passage to the Father which Christ has accomplished in his own flesh. Once we have accepted the call to follow, and do so, we can be made ready to be sent with this gift to others.

Chapter Three

Learning to be a disciple

It may seem to us, as we look over the years of our discipleship that we have changed in many ways, that we have 'come a long way' as we would say. But as T.S. Eliot said, "In my beginning is my end."[1] Whatever form it takes in the historical circumstances unique to each of us, our faith journey never leads us away from but always more deeply into that first point of awakening when faith first stirred in us. The Living God has touched us in our deepest hearts but we live superficial lives on the periphery of the greatest realities and the journey leads us to the central mystery. In the immortal words of St. Augustine, "Late have I loved you, O Beauty ever ancient, ever new, late have I loved you. You were within me, but I was outside and it was there that I searched for you. You called, you shouted, and you broke through my deafness... You breathed your fragrance on me; I drew in my breath and now I pant for you".[2]

This is the mystery that Nathanael was invited to begin to recognise in his first meeting with the man, Jesus of Nazareth and what each of us must discover: even here and now, our lives are 'hidden with Christ in God'.[3] The call to discipleship is a call to live by faith in a present reality beyond all human wisdom to discover but we have to be content to move from where we are to where we are called only as He who calls us thinks fit.

The English expression 'trying to run before you can walk' describes an impatience in us to reach our goal, impatience with the rate of natural growth. The only way we can humanly become what as yet we are not is by unavoidable stages of growth. In so far as we are physical, these stages have an unalterable pattern. They begin at conception and there is no other way to become a human being. In so far as we are rational, there are patterns of emotional and intellectual growth through which we become mature. In so far as we are spiritual, there are also patterns of change and growth that cannot be avoided. To imagine that in the moment we assent to the life of faith we have reached the goal would be very childish indeed.

As people called to faith in God's revelation of himself in the person of Jesus Christ how do we learn to live the life to which we are called? I want to express my understanding of this matter by using an expression which may seem rather odd. My suggestion is that we can imagine that in the life of every disciple of Christ that there is, what I call, an 'Old Testament' period and a 'New Testament' period.

In the way I see things, there is a parallel between what happens on the widest scale with what happens on the smallest scale; the story of mankind's relationship with God to which the Bible testifies on the grandest scale is the story of each person's relationship with God. This being so, the advent of the Word Incarnate did not happen fortuitously; it was not an accident of time and place but, as the Scriptures attest, it occurred "in the fullness of time". In the unfolding of God's plan for all mankind, it occurred no sooner and no later than the right moment. The same thing happens in the life of each believer. In our answering God's call, there comes the moment, not too soon and not too late, when we recognise that, hidden from our eyes though it be, we are alive in Christ.

The historical preparation of Israel for the moment of Christ's advent was not an accident but a necessary stage in the accomplishment of God's purpose. What happened later sprang out of what happened earlier. We have understood nothing about God's revelation and the accomplishing of his purpose in Jesus Christ if we think the Old Testament is old hat. As St. Augustine said, "The new covenant is hidden in the old; the old is revealed in the new".[4] And St. Jerome, his contemporary, commenting on the words of Jesus, "You erred, not knowing the Scriptures and not knowing the power of God" said, in reference to the Old Testament, "Ignorance of Scripture is ignorance of Christ".[5] Our awakening to the life of faith has a history and a future; it occurs 'in the fullness of time' and the One who calls us draws us through patterns of development which we may discern in Sacred Scripture. We learn to appreciate the spiritual reality of the Christian calling through our prayerful attention to the Old Testament.

If I may be so bold as to try and say in one paragraph what God and his inspired authors said in many books over many centuries, I would say this. We are indeed created in the image and likeness of God but we know from daily experience that we are caught up in a mystery of evil we do not begin to understand. In our desire to escape from it, we gladly acknowledge the truth and beauty of moral laws. Indeed, we strive to keep them but we have to learn that the Law has no power to free us from our deep rooted entanglement in sin's mystery. It is as if we try to use the Law to perfect ourselves only to discover that the way to the One who calls us does not lie there. We have to look deep and deeper yet within our hearts and discover two liberating truths.

The first truth describes the ground on which we must ever stand before him who summons us: we can bring nothing to God but a humble and contrite heart. The only power that can bring us to this point is our awakening to the even deeper truth: God has never sought anything else from his beloved, estranged children!

Were I to try and describe, in a nutshell the history of Israel testified to in the Old Testament, I would speak of an initial joy and enthusiasm in being called into covenant and the subsequent discovery that, People of God though it be, it had no power in itself to keep faith with the Covenant. It tried coming to God bringing sacrifices and offerings but had to discover their futility. This pattern of assent to our calling, trying to answer in our own power, failing and learning to come with nothing but a contrite heart is the discovery that each Christian believer must make.

The Old Testament is proclaimed in our worship today not to remind us only of the historical origins of the Church. Its more important role is to teach us about the origins now, in each one of us, of an authentic relationship to God in Christ. Christian prayer today is grounded in the psalms and prayers of the people of the Old Covenant because we too can, and must, say what they said. For this reason one of my favourite prayers of the entire Old Testament is one the Church makes its own in the Liturgy of the Hours. There is a sense in which I wish to come before God in no other company than the people that has been enabled by his grace to say to him: "Blessed are you, O Lord, God of our fathers and worthy of praise and your name is glorified for ever. You are just in all that you have done to us for we have sinned and lawlessly departed from you and have sinned in all things. For your name's sake do not give us up utterly, and do not break your covenant. Do not withdraw your mercy from us for the sake of Abraham your beloved and for the sake of Isaac your servant and Israel your holy one, to whom you promised to make their descendants as many as the stars of heaven and as the sand on the shore of the sea. For we, O Lord, have become fewer than any nation and are brought low this day in all the world because of our sins; and at this time there is no prince, or prophet, or leader, no burnt offering, or sacrifice, or oblation, or incense, no place to make an offering before you or to find mercy. Yet with a contrite heart and a humble spirit, may we be accepted, as though it were with burnt offerings of rams and bulls and with tens of thousands of fat lambs. Such may our sacrifice be in your sight this day and may we wholly follow you, for there will be no shame for those who trust in you. And now with all our heart we follow you, we fear you and seek your face."[6]

In these inspired words, we hear Israel brought not just to its knees but prostrate, having nothing but God's promise and the gift of faith in that promise. In these words, if we can indeed make them our own, we shall find that by God's unfailing kindness he has indeed brought us to what I call 'square one of the Gospel', those first words in which the Lord Jesus announced the coming of the Kingdom, "Repent and believe the good news". This moment is never a moment in the past we grow out of, but as we learn more about the meaning of our calling, it becomes the ever enduring foundation of life in Christ. To lead people to this moment is the purpose of the Catechumenate. This was the pastoral programme which became standardised in the ancient church through which people, already believers, converts to the Gospel of Christ, were prepared to embrace the sacramental life and mission of the Church. It was a preparation that was never rushed.

The formation did not lead believers away from their initial assent to the Gospel rather it led them into the mystery of their having been called. It spelled out for them the consequences of this divine call in terms of beliefs, morals and religious observances. However it did not speak to them about the Sacraments themselves. During the long period of preparation, it was the responsibility of those directing the Catechumenate to assess the progress of each believer, to discern when the right moment had come for them to pass from being only listeners of the Word to become sharers in the sacramental reality their calling was leading them to. Today's Rite of Christian Initiation of Adults is emphatic about the discernment priests and catechists must exercise in this matter.

The Rite of Election that precedes the catechumen's Lenten preparation for Easter Night is a celebration of what I earlier called our Ecclesial vocation that is believed to concretise our Divine vocation. Is it fair to say that many people baptised in infancy have no real awareness of having been called and chosen for that grace in which they stand? Without this awareness, it is most unlikely that anyone will be very conscious of the indescribable privilege of sharing in 'The Mystery of Faith' and lacking this sense, any sense of being sent with so precious a gift to others.

THE CATECHUMENATE

In the year 387, St. Ambrose, bishop of Milan, baptised the thirty-three year old philosophy teacher who was to become St. Augustine, bishop of Hippo. That was a long time ago and the Church has changed a lot since then but we still have, even to this day, an example of the teaching Ambrose gave those who had recently been initiated as Christians: those newly baptised, confirmed and admitted to the Holy Eucharist on Easter Night. He began his catechesis in these words, reminding them of the intense training they had experienced in the preceding months or perhaps years:

"We gave a daily instruction on right conduct when the readings were taken from the history of the patriarchs or the maxims of Proverbs. These readings were intended to instruct and train you, so that you might grow accustomed to the ways of our forefathers, entering into their paths and walking in their footsteps, in obedience to God's commands. Now the *(Easter)* season reminds us that we must speak of the mysteries, setting forth the meaning of the sacraments. If we had thought fit to teach these things to those not yet initiated through baptism, we should be considered traitors rather than teachers. *(but apart from that)* The light of the mysteries is of itself more effective where people do not know what to expect than where some instruction has been given beforehand."[7]

Does it shock you to know that these people during their long period of training had no experience of the Eucharist or other sacraments? Clearly, because they were believers, they were admitted to the Christian assembly, but only as listeners, during the Liturgy of the Word. They were given no clue as to what the assembly did after they were dismissed - which they were before the Eucharist began. However, while they were given no knowledge of the sacraments, they were constantly instructed about God's power revealed in those events and persons in the history of Israel which the Church understood as promises of what was to come. The catechumenate was indeed an 'Old Testament' stage for Christians in the ancient Church. Furthermore, this kind of preparation was regarded as an indispensable formation for anyone wishing to share its life and mission. It continues to be an indispensable formation: one way or another, it has to take place in our lives. At some stage, before we are initiated as adults or after our initiation if we were baptised in infancy we must grow through the experiences the catechumenate offered believers in the early church.

Because we have grown up in a Church which seemed to place baptism as something to be achieved as soon as possible, as the only way to sharing what the Church offers, there is an aspect of the Catechumenate we can easily mistake. Catechumens were not regarded as outside the church and the Catechumenate was not a mission to unbelievers. On the contrary, nobody qualified to be enrolled as catechumens until they had become believers in the Gospel of Jesus. Their position was simply that they had not yet come to that point in their faith journey where they were regarded as being capable of recognising the Living Christ in the concrete reality which is Christ's Church. They will certainly have reached that point where, believing that God's salvation was being offered them in Christ, they realised that it was through the Church's ministry that they were being offered it. This is fine, but it falls far short of the faith that is needed to recognise the indissoluble bond between the Risen Lord Jesus and his bride, the Church. It falls far short of the realisation that there is no Christ without his Body, the Church. This is the great Mystery of Faith which we can only truly be aware of by participation. Sharing in the sacraments, after due catechesis, enables us to believe in this unity between Christ and his members.

Think for a moment of the disciples on the way to Emmaus. Consider what happened to them and one may begin to realise why what the Catechumenate offered people not yet admitted to the Sacraments of Faith has to be experienced by those baptised as infants but who are, as yet, psychologically catechumens.

The disciples on the road to Emmaus had reached some point in their faith with regard to Jesus of Nazareth. Even at this stage, as they walked along the road, the Living Jesus was their teacher although they did not know it. Who instructed the catechumens? It was Christ living in his Church addressing them through those who carried out his mission. Just as one of the purposes of the Catechumenate was to enable believers to reach that point where they could see that Jesus fulfilled all God's promises in the Old Testament, so too, the disciples on the road were accompanied by the Living Lord Jesus who lifted a veil from their minds and hearts. As the concrete reality of his teaching enabled them to grow beyond what they thought they already knew about God's call to faith, so the experience of being catechised within the community of faith enabled catechumens to grow in the faith. Once they experienced the living presence of Jesus in the Sacraments of Initiation, as the disciples recognised him in the breaking of bread, they grasped in a new way all that had been happening to them during the earlier period of their formation. "Did our hearts not burn within us as he talked to us on the road and explained the Scriptures to us?"[8] The disciples on the road, the catechumens and very many baptized in infancy must make the same discovery. Indeed, for believers baptised in infancy, the awakening to the fact that the Risen Christ has been accompanying them at every step of the journey is what enables them to pass from an 'Old Testament' to a 'New Testament' experience of faith.

FORMATION FOR BOTH DISCIPLESHIP AND APOSTLESHIP

If it is so important, why did the Catechumenate fall into disuse and why did the Second Vatican Council say that it "must be restored"? The answer lies in the way we think of the Church and our place in it.

There came a time in our history when it was assumed that the European nations had been evangelised. The ground had been prepared and the Church built up. People were born into a social entity known as 'Christendom': a marriage between Church (meaning the hierarchy) and organs of State (meaning the rule of Emperor or monarch). This was the Europe that endured until the Protestant Reformation. In what was assumed to be a Christian society, clergy were seen as responsible for its spiritual well-being and lay people for its temporal welfare. In so far as the Church had a mission to accomplish, it was the clergy's prerogative to shepherd souls to heaven and the laity, busy about the affairs of this world, were passengers in the Barque of Peter. 'Missionaries' were clergy sent to places where the Church had yet to be established.

This being so, the sacraments came to be seen less as sacred signs incorporating people into the Body of Christ on earth to share in its life and mission but more as events 'administered' to individuals by the clergy for their individual well-being in the next life. Even in 1939, Pope Pius XI spoke of Catholic Action as "the participation of the laity in the hierarchical apostolate of the Church".[9] The Second Vatican Council broke through this tradition to a much more ancient understanding of the Church and this, I believe is one of the reasons the Council said that the Catechumenate must be restored. The Catechumenate formed people not only for discipleship; they were already disciples; they also had to be prepared for mission.

A pastoral institution, the Catechumenate recognised that there are authentic disciples of Christ whose development has not sufficiently matured for them to make a total commitment to the life and work of Christ. Throughout their years or months as catechumens these disciples were taught the moral law, the need for prayer, the need to seek the will of God with all their hearts. They were prayed with and anointed that God would strengthen them; they were promised in Christ's name the power to persevere. But here comes the Christian paradox.

The same catechetical process which taught them the beauty and glory of living by God's Law, taught them to engage in prayerful reflection on what they experienced within themselves. Experience of their constant shortcomings brought them to that point where their faith was purified of any illusory self-righteousness. This would enable them to confess that they brought to God nothing but their sinfulness, their contrite hearts and the realisation that they needed God's gift to take even their first steps in the life of faith. The Catechumenate led them to that point where, relying totally on the power of God, they turned away forever from the life they had hitherto lived and made their commitment to God's promise in the crucified and risen Christ. Only when they had renounced sin and turned to Christ with a life commitment were they thought ready, only then were they led, physically, where they had never been before, to experiences of which they had no prior knowledge.

Conversion to a whole-hearted commitment preceded Christian Initiation. For those of us baptised as infants incapable of faith or love, initiation preceded conversion but conversion there must be to both the life and mission of the church otherwise we remain, psychologically, catechumens. We have to undergo, in whatever form it takes, the formation that enables us to make a mature commitment to the living Lord Jesus, so we can know the power of his commitment to us, which is nothing less than the gift of His Spirit living in us through our sacramental communion with Him.

SACRAMENTS OF THE OLD AND NEW COVENANTS

Being alive to the abiding presence of the Holy Spirit is the difference between what I am calling 'Old Testament' and 'New Testament' living. If we consider some of the 'sacred signs' of the old covenant, which Thomas Aquinas had no problem in calling 'sacraments',[10] we shall soon realise the difference between them and the sacraments of the new and eternal covenant. I venture to use language here that cannot be said to be theologically accurate but gives some idea of the difference. The crossing of the sea, the journey to Sinai, the Law written on stone tablets, the manna, the cloud of God's presence, the tent of meeting, the Levitical priesthood, the rite of entering the Holy of Holies, all these may be said to have been signs of grace but they did nothing to change the inner man. They were, in my own language, 'outward signs of outward grace' whereas the sacred signs of the new covenant are classically known as 'outward signs of inward grace'. All these material, physical events and objects were simply promises yet to be fulfilled; signs and promises of what would be real *spiritual* realities which change human beings in the depths of their being and which for this reason are absolutely and totally the object of faith.

We say that in Christian Initiation, what happens to the individual believer in sacred sign is a participation in what happened to the humanity of Jesus in his dying and rising. To use the sacred sign language of the old covenant, each human being who has been incorporated into Jesus in his dying and rising, is now in living communion with the Living God in the Holy of Holies. What in the world can be more sacred than that? "Did you not know," says St. Paul, "that *you* are the temple of God and that the Spirit of God dwells in you?"[11] Living as members of the sacramental reality which is Christ's Body on earth, is to live a life so utterly the object of faith that St. Paul says of it, "You have died and your lives are hidden, with Christ in God."[12]

The Bible as a whole testifies to the cosmic dimensions of the History of Salvation but at the same time, witnesses to the fact that this divine/human reality must exist in each person. This is how the Kingdom of God is established in creation. Writing of the entire grand sweep of this salvation history 'in a nutshell' I was reminded of Julian of Norwich. "He shewed me," she says, "a little thing, the quantity of a hazel nut, lying in the palm of my hand and to my understanding it was as round as any ball. I looked thereupon and thought, "What may this be?" And I was answered thus "It is all that is made." I marvelled how it could last, for methought it might fall suddenly to naught for littleness. And I was answered: "It lasts and ever shall because God loves it, and so hath all thing its being through the love of God."[13]

All mankind and each one of us is caught in the mystery of sin but with the freedom the contrite heart brings, we awaken to the infinitely greater mystery of the love which embraces all that is. In this awakening we realise that not only are we a forgiven people, not only are we a healed people we are people restored to that image and likeness to God for which we were first created. We have, in Jesus Christ crucified and risen, been raised to a communion with God that is not the object of sense, sentiment, feeling, or rational analysis, but is entirely the object of faith. Living in this faith is what I have called the 'New Testament' period in our lives and it begins when we awaken to the reality of our Christian Initiation.

Chapter Four

Christian Initiation

Most of us have grown up in a fairly comfortable, unpersecuted Church. Indeed, until recent decades it was still considered a respectable thing to be a church-goer in our country. In this church infant baptism is regarded as the norm, even though the faith of those seeking the baptism of their infants can be very tenuous indeed. This is followed by admitting to Holy Communion a whole class of school children, just because they have reached the age of seven, even though many, sometimes the majority, will have had little or no experience of Mass – except at school. The finishing touch to this failed pastoral approach is celebrated in what has been cynically called the sacrament of departure: teenage confirmation. There is plenty of evidence of vibrant faith among many young adults but it is also a sad fact that exposure to things 'Catholic' in childhood and adolescence is not producing in the majority of those thus exposed signs of faith and commitment.

Mere knowledge of the Catholic doctrine is not the same as the life-giving Good News about the free salvation that the Living Lord Jesus offers believers in the concrete realities we call the Sacraments. They may well have learned that Jesus 'instituted' the sacraments, they may have been able to recite what in Scholastic theology was called the 'matter and form' of each; they may have learned that the personal holiness or otherwise of the minister effect in no way the efficacy of the Sacraments. They may have been able to say that there are three persons in one God; that as God, Jesus Christ is everywhere, as God made man he is in heaven and in the sacrament of the altar. All this is sound Catholic Doctrine. However, if in receiving this information, they gained no sense of the awesome mystery in which they were personally involved by God's own invitation and free gift, the information did them no good at all.

Indeed, if their experience of being taught these things was an experience only of human power over others, rather than an apostle's desire to share an undeserved gift, the information was probably counter productive. If coupled with all this, the mystery of our calling to follow Christ was reduced to a command to obey moral and ecclesiastical laws at the peril of one's immortal soul, it is not surprising that we may conclude that they were not evangelised. If they lapsed, from what did they lapse? And if they are to be recalled, to what are they to be converted? You can't give what you don't have and any church that settles for this situation is in no position to become an evangelising church for it is itself in sore need of catechising and even evangelising. On the contrary it is well on the way to extinction. I once heard a bishop speaking with great insight, about 'baptising a lapsed church'.

How very different things were in the ancient church when during three centuries of repeated persecutions Christians grew from a handful of people into a communion of numerous Churches spread all across the Mediterranean world. In this ancient Church there was no rush to admit people to the Sacraments of Faith. The Church was content to instruct and form people for as long as it took to bring them to that faith which would enable them to live with eagerness and joy the Church's sacramental life and share in its mission. When they were finally deemed ready they were prepared to take part in the Church's sacramental celebration of Christ's Paschal Mystery on Easter Night.

In the days preceding, they had been given treasures previously unknown to them: the Symbol of Faith. What we call the Creed, shared by all the churches throughout the world, was imparted to them for the first time. They had to learn it by heart and 'give it back' by proclaiming it aloud. We still have St. Augustine's homily for the occasion in which he encourages them not be afraid of faltering in their reply because they would not find him a stern school master. After this they were given, to be their very own, that which belongs only to the sons and daughters of God: the Lord's own prayer. Finally after all the anointings, exorcisms and prayers that had accompanied them throughout the Catechumenate, there took place the "Ephphatha" – "Be opened". In this sacred rite, the Church repeated with each of them what the Lord Jesus had done for the man born deaf and dumb[1] undoing that terrible deafness to the word of God spoken of by the prophet Isaiah[2] freeing them to receive the full impact of Mysteries they were to experience.

In the darkness of the night with the aid of deacons and deaconesses, they prepared themselves for what lay ahead not knowing what that was. Stripped of their clothes, shivering perhaps with nothing but a cloak around them, they faced the brooding darkness of the Western sky and renounced Satan and all his works. To celebrate their freedom, they were invited to make some defiantly rude gesture - blowing a raspberry was the way one writer has written about it.[3] Then they turned their back forever on all that had entangled them in sin, proclaiming towards the dawning light of the Eastern sky, their commitment to the Lord Jesus Christ. Remember, they made this commitment not with any knowledge of the power of the Spirit which was to be imparted to them in the Sacraments. They knew nothing of all this. The Catechumenate had enabled them to face and to accept their weakness and helplessness: they had come to accept their need for redemption and Jesus as their redeemer. Charismatics talk about arriving at this point where one 'steps out with expectant faith'. I once heard a preacher speaking about the same reality, using a different vocabulary. He said, "Once the commitment is made, the providence of God follows on." This, I believe, is what was asked of the Catechumens: to make an irrevocable commitment to Jesus Christ as Lord and having done so, they would experience the power of his grace.

Only when they had come to this point in their discipleship were they led out of the dark into the blazing lights of the Baptistry. There they were to experience the Christian 'mysteries'; the 'concrete realities penetrated by the Divine Presence' which we call the 'sacraments'.

Having professed their faith they were led down into waters that submerged them and from there they were raised up in the name of the Father, the Son and the Holy Spirit. In sacred sign they passed with Christ through death and the tomb and, reconciled to the Father were raised to a new life in the Spirit. After this, having been clothed in white garments, sweet–smelling perfume was outpoured upon their heads, and they were 'Christened' anointed with the Spirit for mission. New living members of Christ they were led into the assembly of the faithful to acclamations that "Christ is Risen!" Here, for the first time in their lives they saw the bread and wine brought to the altar and heard the Risen Lord's words to them "Take and eat, this is my Body." "Take and drink this is the cup of my blood, the blood of the new and everlasting covenant."

Having made their commitment to God in Christ, they now found that he had made an everlasting commitment to them. Then, at the end when the assembly was dismissed, they too were sent sharing the mission of that whole company whose witness had brought them this moment, "Go!" "Ite, missa est".

At last, the catechumens were permitted to take their place in what the Lord had been calling them to. It was in a church of such great conviction that countless numbers were able to sacrifice their lives rather than deny Christ in communion with whom they had already overcome death. The Catechumenate trained them well and they were able to give up their lives on earth because of the conviction they had about the unseen, unfelt, spiritual reality of their life in Christ.

LIVING BY FAITH THE SACRAMENTAL LIFE

This spiritual reality is not some airy-fairy, pie-in-the sky-when-you-die. The whole meaning of 'sacrament' or 'mystery' is that it is a here and now concrete reality of flesh and blood human beings who embody the spiritual. It is evident that in our Catholic Christian worship we do not despise the physical, the material. How can we, when in our worship we are for ever using water, oil, bread and wine? So in what I say now, it would be a mistake to imagine that I decry our use of material objects, our dedicating them to the celebration of our worship or the desire to ensure that our worship is beautiful in what is seen and heard. Nevertheless, we have to move from an Old Testament to a New Testament understanding of what they signify.

Is a building that has been dedicated to the worship of God, however splendidly built, more sacred than even the most humble member of Christ? Is a chalice more holy than the sacred sign it is intended to bear and is that sacred sign more sacred than the human being it exists to nourish? The question is do we live by faith in the spiritual reality embodied in real people or by projection of this mystery onto physical objects?

How much less challenging it can be to project outside ourselves the sacred, an essentially interior, spiritual reality gracing human beings, and placing it on a pedestal out there, in music and ceremonial, rather than to look about you at Mass and seeing the ordinary, the smelly, the noisy, the ugly, and recognise 'here is the Living Christ' I repudiate this pre-Gospel tendency in all of us, with all my heart. The sacred may be reflected in the beauty of music and ritual, but God does not live in any kind of house, however beautiful, made by human hands. The 'concrete reality penetrated by the Divine Presence' is *people*, the living company of human beings who are the One Body of Christ on earth. It is to this object of faith that all the Liturgical reforms of the Second Vatican Council call us. I see it as a failure to recognise this challenge, the retreat into earlier liturgical traditions, humanly appealing splendours that disguised this truth. The Letter to the Hebrews drawing on the making of the old covenant invites us to look with faith on what has happened in this concrete, historical world through our sacramental union with the crucified and risen Christ.

"You have not approached that which could be touched and a blazing fire and gloomy darkness and storm and a trumpet blast and a voice speaking words such that those who heard begged that no message be further addressed to them for they could not bear the commandment, 'If even an animal touches the mountain, it shall be stoned'. Indeed, so fearful was the spectacle that Moses said, 'I am terrified and trembling.' No, you have come to Mount Zion and the city of the living God, the heavenly Jerusalem and countless angels in festal gathering, and the assembly of the first-born enrolled in heaven and God the judge of all and the spirits of the just made perfect and Jesus the mediator of a new covenant and the sprinkled blood that speaks more eloquently than that of Abel."[4]

We do not live in the age of promises as yet to be fulfilled. We live in the age of the 'sacred sign of reconciliation between God and man and among mankind'[5] accomplished for all mankind in the death and resurrection of Jesus. We live in the age of the Church, living members of the Body of Christ. We are part of a sacramental reality existing even now in this world that is on its way to a fulfilment beyond human history. But what is the source of this spiritual life we lead, which must be the focus of our life of faith? It is nothing less than the fulfilment of the greatest promise made through the prophets of the Old Testament. The promise that was fulfilled when the Risen Lord Jesus breathed upon the assembled disciples imparting to them life by which he now lives, and said, "Receive the Holy Spirit."[6]

God has touched us, awakening us to the reality of what perhaps we thought we already believed in: the spiritual reality of the Spirit outpoured in us, ordinary, weak, real people living in the real world. We have but to awaken in faith, and believing, act. It is in our ordinary daily lives that living by faith is put to the test. In our discipleship we live with disappointments, failures, set-backs and what seem to be successes. Human wisdom is not the judge of their true measure. All must be submitted to the Mystery of Faith, for our lives are hidden with Christ in God and that means they are hidden even from our own sight! We honour the God who has called us to live in his presence if we can offer him that act of worship we give the Lord Jesus in the greatest sign of his presence: "Oh Godhead hid, profoundly I adore Thee who truly art within the forms before me."

We begin our discipleship, it seems to me, ready to believe things about God, his Christ and what he has done in the world. This I call the 'Old Testament' part of our story. At the providential moment, it is given us to realise the immanence of all that we thought we believed God was doing. The story, the History of Salvation from the story of Adam to the image of Jerusalem taken up into Heaven as God's Bride, is my story. The story of all is the story of each. It is the object of faith 'a stumbling block to the Jews *(Israel)* and foolishness to Gentiles. But to those who are called, Christ the power of God and the wisdom of God.[7]

Chapter Five

As the Father sent me, I am sending you

Called and sent, we live our following of Christ in the power of his Spirit outpoured, his presence in our lives, the object of our faith. No less the object of the profoundest faith is the presence of Spirit in our being sent. Unless we take this to heart and ponder it deeply, we shall spend a long time trying to do in our own power what we cannot do. We can, and must bring our natural gifts and acquired skills to our service of Christ and his Church but it is another thing altogether, to remember that we must submit them to the Spirit's anointing and leadership. However, more important than any natural talents we offer are the Spirit's charismatic gifts. It is a wonderful thing indeed, to integrate all our natural talents into our Christian calling but even more wonderful to be open to those supernatural gifts which the Spirit alone can give for the building up of the Church. The Second Vatican Council taught this doctrine quite explicitly.[1]

In order to appreciate what the Council affirmed about the existence and need for these gifts, we have to bear in mind that prior to the Council it was a common opinion that these manifestations of the Spirit's sovereign presence in the Church were particular to the earliest days of the early church but not subsequently. It was thought that with the manifestation (or as we may say nowadays, with a profound degree of truth) the evolution of the institutional gifts, the free gifts were no longer needed.

THE ANOINTING OF THE SPIRIT ENDURES

The Living Lord Jesus breathes into us the very Spirit of God, sending us in the power of the Spirit as he was sent by the Father. Just as the catechumens, like Israel before them, had to find by experience that only in the gift of the Spirit can anyone keep faith with the Covenant, so too, we have to find out that it is only in the power of the Spirit that we can do anything to accomplish the mission entrusted to us. If it is only in the power of the invisible Spirit that we can live the Christian life; it is only in the power of the same Spirit that we can act in Christ's name, to bring others to him.

Jesus, returning to his home town after being baptised in the Spirit, proclaimed the Sacred Scripture before all who knew him as their local carpenter. In the words of the prophet Isaiah, he announced, "The Spirit of the Lord is upon me, because he has anointed me to bring glad tidings to the poor. He has sent me to proclaim liberty to captives and recovery of sight to the blind, to let the oppressed go free, and to proclaim a year acceptable to the Lord."[2] Like Nathanael who, when confronted with the words of Jesus, had to bring two concrete realities together, Jesus' neighbours faced a huge challenge to faith as someone they had known since childhood said of himself, "Today, this scripture passage is fulfilled in your hearing."[3] The same challenge faces every person baptised in their infancy for we are faced with the challenge of believing that each person baptised in the name of the Father, Son and Holy Spirit has been anointed prophet, to bear witness to the Living God and his Christ.

EVANGELISATION

If we are to fulfil our privileged calling, there is a certain notion about evangelisation we need to dispose of. Just as some Christians think that the books of the Old Testament are about nothing more than the past, so there are those who imagine that Gospel preaching is nothing more than a historical task to be accomplished as a one-off event in the history of some region before the Church can be established there. This idea suggests that once the institutions of the Church have been set up, the work of evangelising has been completed. Evangelisation is indeed a ground-breaking exercise, an indispensable, foundation-building task, which makes possible that sharing in the life of the Church described in the last chapter. However, what has to happen to all, has to happen to each! Evangelisation is required not only by a first generation of believers, it is needed by each believer in every generation.

It is evident that if the church is to exist in a place where it has never existed before, the Gospel must be both proclaimed and received there. However, this proclaiming and receiving of the Gospel continues to be the essential foundation of the Church's continued existence. Each new generation of the People of God has to hear and receive the Gospel. Each generation has to be evangelised. Indeed, each person in every generation has to be evangelised if the People of God is to accomplish its mission in any particular place and moment in history.

Where the Gospel is not proclaimed and received, such pastoral work as the institutional church carries out cannot produce its fruit. The situation may even arise where members of the Church in a certain region or country imagine that they are 'born' Catholics and that 'converts' are people born outside the clan. It may even be imagined that people baptised in infancy do not themselves have to be converted. Even worse, such instruction as they are given might even give the impression that Catholic doctrine is the same thing as the Gospel of Christ and that to have a knowledge of doctrine is to have heard and received the Gospel of Christ. Where this happens, there exists that caricature of Church which for decades has been described by some European bishops as a people sacramentalised but not evangelised. A generation that has received only information about God's purpose in Christ (doctrine) is not equipped to be an evangelising church.

We must take in the terrible indictment of this judgment. It is not merely a rather unfortunate thing that there exist local churches where people have been admitted to the sacraments but have never been converted to the Glad Tidings of Jesus; it is a major scandal, a disaster. For it means that unless these people are evangelised, the Church, like the seed scattered on the rocky ground, will wither for lack of roots.[4] Lest we mistake the import of what is being said here, we must distinguish two distinct elements in the Church's mission, evangelisation and catechesis. As I understand it, catechesis is the process of Christian formation that must continue throughout our discipleship. Certainly there is a particular catechesis required for Christian Initiation but that is just the beginning of a life-long process. Catechesis builds on something assumed to have already taken place, namely that the person being formed in the Christian way of life, by being exposed to the Church's rich tradition in this matter, has already turned aside from all that does not lead to God and has awoken to the immanence of God's call to them in Jesus Christ.

Evangelisation is the enduring foundation on which all Christian formation and practice is based, precisely because *to come to faith in the person of Jesus is to establish a completely new foundation upon which one's life is built*. This simple fact is the very core of evangelisation. It has to be said that there are those in the Roman Catholic Church, and, I have no doubt, those born into other Christian traditions to whom the words of the prophet Elijah apply: "How long will you straddle this issue? If the Lord is God, follow him; if Baal, follow him." [5] Whether a person comes to this life-changing choice before or after Christian Initiation is not the issue here. What has to be clearly understood is that it has to happen if there is to be any lasting Christian formation. When I said that at the age of nineteen, I experienced a call to 'adult Christian faith', this is precisely what I meant. I was invited to make a choice that altered the direction my life took. In saying that our Christian calling does not lead us away from but ever more deeply into our initial calling, I am saying that our initial evangelisation must take ever deeper roots in our personality.

EVANGELISATION AND CATECHESIS

Catechesis then, is distinct from evangelisation. Successful catechesis is build upon evangelisation. While it involves instruction in Catholic Doctrine and practice, this element by no means exhausts its purpose. For some time in our fairly recent history, 'convert instructions', as any catechism of the period could show, actually mean little more than a sharing of information. It offered a comprehensive and articulate summary of Catholic Doctrine and assent to this, so it seems, made one a Catholic Christian.

R.C.I.A. makes clear that this is not the case. It speaks of what it calls *'an adequate acquaintance'* with doctrine as an essential part of catechesis and assumes, I think it is safe to say, that what is 'adequate' will surely depend on the circumstances of each person. However, it makes abundantly clear that catechesis must above all things, instil a *'profound sense'* of the mystery the catechumen is going to be involved in by the sacraments of faith.[6] Evangelising, and catechising built on its sure foundation, leads to this profound sense of the Christian Mystery.

I have written of my first experience of this profound sense of the mystery when I was a young teenager. It is what we call the first gift of the Spirit, 'Fear of the Lord.' or, more usually nowadays, 'awe in the presence of the Lord'. Without this gift, the Sacraments of Christian Initiation will not produce their full effect. Catechesis prepares the way for it. Without evangelising, catechesis will be nothing more than information.

How then shall we speak of what it means to have heard the Gospel so that the heart can be awakened through catechesis to the awesome reality of the 'concrete reality penetrated by the Divine Presence' which is Christ' Church? We use the word 'evangelised' to mean that a person has experienced himself being spoken to, called, by the Living God though the Good News of Christ.

To hear this Good News about oneself, and to believe that in the proclamation of this Good News, the Living God is actively and personally approaching you for your eternal well-being is to begin to be evangelised.

To believe that in the Gospel, you are being introduced to the secret of human existence is to begin to be evangelised.

To believe that through the Gospel, what is true on the widest possible, cosmic level is equally true about you, in the depths of your human heart, is to begin to be evangelised.

To believe that there was nothing you could do in your own power to work out this secret, that there was nothing you could do in your own power to cause God to reveal this meaning to you, nothing you could do in your own power to earn the free gift of reconciliation and grace, but that it is indeed happening now, through the Good News of Christ, is to begin to be evangelised.

It is the awesome privilege of every member of the Church to engage in sharing with others this gift.

SHARING THE WORD OF GOD

When the prophets spoke in the name of the Lord, they used such expressions as "Thus says the Lord", "The Lord says this." They were powerfully aware that nobody had the right to stand up and speak for God without having been appointed to the task. If one was appointed to the task, it would have been blasphemous to say, in God's holy name, something one knew to be false or watered down out of human respect for the listeners, or altered to suit one's own agenda not God's. To be a prophet of God was regarded as a most awesome calling. That word again! Awesome. Silence and awe in the presence of the holy.

It speaks in the first place, of the wonder welling up in the heart of the prophet, the one sent, realising that the Lord himself has entrusted to him the honour of his holy name. The Lord has entrusted to him a word that is to turn his people back to him. The Lord has entrusted to him the task of showing people the way they must take if they will return to the Lord.

In the second place, it speaks of the amazement in the heart of the one who hears and believes the prophet's word - the liberating, graceful moment of realisation: God himself has a word for me. He calls me from going my own way, back to himself. He invites me to move forward in a new way.

All this is true of the prophets right up to John the Baptist. The Spirit of God spoke through the Prophets, so proclaims the Creed. The Letter to the Hebrews says, "At various times in the past and in various different ways, God spoke to our ancestors through the prophets but in our own time, the last days, he has spoken to us through his Son."[7] However, the action of the Spirit of God on the prophets of the Old Covenant was never regarded as a permanent outpouring, more a touch, a transitory inspiration. What has changed, with the coming of the New and Eternal Covenant is that the Spirit *rested* upon Jesus and the Risen Jesus himself, established in power, poured out this same Spirit on the whole people he had gathered to himself. St. Paul in the Second Letter to the Corinthians, speaking about the awesome mission entrusted to the Church says, "We are ambassadors for Christ; it is as though God were appealing through us and the appeal that we make in Christ's name is, be reconciled to God."[8]

The empowerment Christ's Church has received to carry out its mission to bring the Good News to all mankind, is not a transitory touch of the Spirit. The Spirit has been poured out upon the whole People of God and this truth is proclaimed in the baptism of each new infant brought into this gathered people. After the water was poured, every one of us baptised in infancy was addressed in these words, "As Christ was anointed, priest, prophet and king, so may you live always as a member of his holy people."[9]

If the vocation of the ancient prophets is awesome and if indeed, John the Baptist, according to the words of Jesus himself was the greatest of them, how much more awesome is the vocation of every member of the Body of Christ, sharing the Lord's own permanent anointing with the Spirit for the service of the Gospel.

We can only give others what we have ourselves consciously received. Only by awakening to the present reality of our own being called by God and being graced by God can we be the bearer to others of God's call to them. Only by being evangelised ourselves can we evangelise others.

EVANGELISING: A HUMANLY IMPOSSIBLE TASK

In our Catholic tradition we have a highly developed sense that there are some things which human beings can do in the name, that is to say, in the power of Jesus Christ which they are incapable of in their own power. The classic example would be our high awareness of the sacramental power of the ordained priest. On the one hand we confess that in celebrating Mass, the ordained priest has a unique role to play in the assembly but on the other, we recognise his power to do so has nothing to do with either his personal, human qualities or his personal goodness or even sanctity. The reality of his sacramental ministry is for us, an object of faith. We believe that the Spirit of God is acting through him. At the heart of our faith, the celebration of the Eucharist, there takes place a human activity which has no meaning for us except that it embodies a divine activity: it is a sacrament.

This word was used about the Church's activities from the most ancient time but in the Middle Ages the word became restricted, used in that special sense we have become used to, referring to seven specific events in the life of the Church This restricted sense has, unfortunately blinded many of us to the much wider, ancient usage. This was the use of the word to which Pope Paul VI was recalling the Church in the phrase I have quoted already from his first address to the Second Vatican Council, "I believe that the Church is a mystery, a sacrament, that is to say, a concrete reality penetrated by the Divine presence." Everything that manifests the Church's true self is a sacramental reality, everything from its first beginnings to its full flowering. The proclaiming of the Gospel is its beginning and this task is a human reality penetrated by the

Divine presence. While it is essentially a human activity, it is also essentially a divine activity. It is something which takes place in this world, the activity of one human being through which the very Word of God is conveyed to and which touches the heart of another human being. Before speaking about this most wonderful thing, I want to attend to the matter of the human qualities we can and should bring to the task.

It should go without saying that our Christian calling does not ignore our human personality with all its qualities and defects. As the Scholastics said, grace builds on nature. If the most basic form of evangelisation is the witness of a Christian life, it will be evident that everything about us should be at the service of our calling. I am reminded of a bishop a few decades ago who had a wide reputation as a very charismatic figure. He once said in my presence referring to his well-known ebullient character, "All that business, everyone thinks it is grace. It's not. It is just the way I am. I am an extrovert. But I have to say this (and I remember vividly the humility with which he said it) I have always tried to put it at the service of the Gospel."

God help us all and God help the mission of the Church if the success of the mission were to depend on certain personality types. We all know how easily we are deceived – this can easily happen in Charismatic circles. Things that are purely human characteristics are taken to be manifestations of the Spirit. "By their fruits you shall know them" said the Lord.[10] Nowadays, just when we are recovering the meaning of the word 'charismatic' as a specific manifestation of the Spirit, it has a currency in everyday language which means nothing more than a powerful human attractiveness.

Perhaps there never was a less charismatic figure, in this sense, than St. John Vianney, the 19th century parish priest of Ars. By all accounts he was a dull plodder even from his youth. His contemporaries and superiors dismissed him as the opposite of a high-flyer or an earth-shaker. However, his memory is honoured as someone whose words, however pathetic a preacher he may have been regarded as by those who know all about 'sacred eloquence', touched human hearts in a way that those who heard, knew they were hearing the Word of God.

By all means let us rejoice to put at the service of the Gospel whatever human qualities we have been endowed with and let us develop them as best we may and may the Spirit grace them too. Some people become very learned and can share their learning with others by lecturing. Some are great teachers, inspiring others with their insights. Some are marvellous at leading discussions, enabling members of the group to articulate and share their insights with others. Let us be ready to put at the service of the Word whatever natural gifts we have of intellect, imagination or style. In all this, however, there is one thing and one thing only which, I believe, disposes us to be at the service of the Spirit and therefore of the Word. This is our readiness to expose ourselves as believers. I am quite convinced that the key to being able to convey the word of God is to forget sharing ideas about God and be ready only to witness to the faith that God has graced you with. The Lord says, "Have no fear. What you are to say at that time will be given to you."[11]

If we are not afraid to stand up in our nakedness, shorn of any attribute which qualifies us in human judgement to be worth listening to, then I do believe we can be begin to be true witnesses to Jesus, it is possible that the Spirit can so grace us that we may indeed be heralds of the Gospel.

THE POWER TO PROCLAIM THE WORD

The gift of the Spirit which enables us to speak the Word of God we call the gift of prophecy. The prophets of God were never called by God see around corners into the future as in a crystal ball. Prophets were not sent to describe what God would do in the future but to proclaim what God wants done now in view of his promises. Prophets are sent to address the present moment. That is why the Lord Jesus promised that his witnesses would be given what they needed to say when called upon to speak in his name.

We have already seen that this gift, under the ancient Covenant, was given intermittently and only to some. You may recall that when this Spirit came down on the handful of assistants to Moses some people complained when one or two not designated began to prophecy as well. Rather than stop them, Moses cried, "Oh! if only the whole people of the Lord were prophets and the Lord gave his Spirit to them all."[12] On the day of Pentecost, St. Peter said, quoting the prophet Joel, that this is precisely what had happened that day.

Deference to those called to pastoral leadership in the Church should not blind us to the fact that while they may also be gifted evangelists and catechists, their pastoral role does not mean they are better qualified than any other baptised person for the task of evangelising or catechising. We know from our experiences in other walks of life that some people make excellent managers but are hopeless on the front line. Think of the difference between care-workers and the director of an aid agency. The ministries are quite different and both are needed but the organisation exists to do what the care-worker is doing not the other way round. Praise God for the enduring way many bishops have exercised their responsibility to teach but having said that, even an enclosed nun who died in her twenties has been hailed as someone who has something to say which benefits the whole Church: St.Therese of Lisieux, Doctor of the Church.

Each believer has to awaken to his or her calling as an evangelist, the bringer of good news. Each believer has to awaken to the anointing they have received. Each believer has to stir up the gifts that were given. We shall become an evangelising Church when we stop looking to others to do what we ourselves have already been empowered to do - when we stop thinking it is somebody else's job. We must cut through every human judgement about ourselves and our human abilities and bring faith to the situation. We are members of a sacramental reality. The Spirit of God longs to act through us. We must pray for an awakening of the gifts we have been given. The gift of prophecy is given to the whole People.

To bring the good news to someone is a sacramental reality for it is nothing less than a human word which carries the Word of God. It is this great mystery of grace we must turn to now.

THE POWER OF THE WORD

It is said in the Letter to the Hebrews, "The word of God is something alive and active: it cuts like any double-edged sword but more finely. It can slip through the place where the soul is divided from the spirit, or joints from the marrow. It can judge the secret emotions and thoughts. No created thing can hide from him; everything is uncovered and open to the eyes of the one to whom we must give account of ourselves."[13]

These words come after the author's commentary on a verse of psalm 95

> "Oh that today you would listen to his voice,
> harden not your hearts as at Meribah
> as on that day at Massah in the desert
> when your fathers put me to the test
> when they tried me, though they saw my work."

Massah and Meribah stand as an archetypal moment in Israel's history. Repeated reference to this event throughout the Old Testament confesses utter dismay at Israel's constant attitude to the word God spoke to his people "at various times and in different ways through the prophets." The insulting test to which the Lord was subjected at Massah and throughout the Old Testament was, "Is the Lord with us or not?" - What deep, deep hurt is contained in the words, "They tried me even though they had seen my works". They could not believe the word by which the Lord had revealed himself to every single person called to speak and act in his name, "I will be with you." Abraham, Moses, David and all the prophets, however inadequate to the task they felt themselves to be, were given this word, "I will be with you".

It is precisely this promise that Jesus, the Word made flesh, gave to those he sent in his name, "Go, proclaim the Good News to all nations - I will be with you even to the end of the world."[14] Every day, at the beginning of the Church's Daily prayer, we are invited to recite psalm 95 for we are not different from any other person called into the People of God since its first beginnings. There is no way we can be an evangelising church and no way can anyone of us become an evangelist if we do not live with a lively faith in the word, "I will be with you." Whether we are talking about our personal struggles to live as followers of the Lord Jesus or whether we are talking about our efforts to carry out our apostolic mission, at every turn, at every breath we need to remember, "I am with you".

"Without me you can do nothing."[15]

"I tell you solemnly; whoever believes in me will perform the same works as I do myself. He will perform even greater works, because I am going to the Father."[16]

What is this work that we shall be able do? It is to bear through our human activities, that Divine reality which can reach into someone else's deepest self, to be able to touch another where only God himself can reach. This touch is the beginning and the end of evangelisation.

BEARERS OF THE WORD

Baldwin of Canterbury, a 12th. Century archbishop has something memorable to say about this. Commenting on the passage "The word of God is alive and active; it cuts like a double-edged sword," he says,

"In this passage, the word of God is plainly shown in all its strength and wisdom to those who seek out Christ who is himself the word, the power and wisdom of God. The word was with the Father in the beginning and at its own time was revealed to the apostles then preached by them and humbly received in faith by believers. The word, then, is in the bosom of the father, in the mouth of the preacher and in the heart of the believer."[17]

Contemplate with faith and awe this mystery, that each member of the People of God is called and empowered to convey from the heart of the Father to the heart of the believer, the word that gives life. The Lord Jesus said that John the Baptist was the greatest of all the prophets God had sent his people, but that to be the least in the Kingdom, whose coming the Gospel proclaims, is to be greater. This is not to deny the veneration due to this saint of God, traditionally honoured second only to the Blessed Virgin. It is not the dedication to the vocation which is the point but the nature of the vocation.

The high point of John's calling came when he pointed away from himself, sending people away to go after Jesus, "Behold the Lamb of God."[18] The Church would betray its calling werc it to do this. At the heart of its life, it points only within itself proclaiming, "Behold the Lamb of God". All evangelists and catechists share in the task of leading believers to this faith by which the Church lives and is sent.

St. Augustine, commenting on the symbolism of John's birth offers us, with his accustomed subtlety, an image to ponder in reference to our own vocation. He says, "Zachary fell silent and lost the power of speech until John, the Lord's precursor, was born and restored his speech. His tongue was loosened because a voice was born. 'I am the voice of one crying in the wilderness' John said of himself. John was a 'voice' but in the beginning the Lord was the Word. John was a voice for a time but Christ, who in the beginning was the Word, is the Word eternally."[19]

St. Jerome, reflecting on God's inspiration in prophets says, very graphically, "It was not the air vibrating with the human voices that reached their ears, but rather it was God speaking within the soul of the prophets".[20]

What a grace! For a while in the historical unfolding of God's purpose for all mankind, it has been given to us, as it was given to the apostles, to convey on the breath of our voices, the eternal Word. We may well be, in the words of St. Paul "only earthenware jars that hold this treasure to make it clear that such an overwhelming power comes from God and not from us."[21] But like Paul, we must be bold with that gift of the Spirit which we call 'courage', and embrace the reality of our calling, for God is indeed with us.

We are then Word-bearers. In this, we share the grace and calling of the Blessed Virgin. This is why she is presented to us as the archetype of the Church. On this subject, Blessed Isaac of Stella, like Baldwin, another English Cistercian of the 12th. century has something remarkable to say. Isaac wishes us to contemplate the grace of God in Mary, the Church and each individual member of the Church. The Church makes his teaching its own for his words are proclaimed in the Office of Readings on the 2nd Saturday of Advent.[22] Whatever the Scriptures say in a general way about the Church, it says in a particular way about Mary and also the other way round, so that when mention is made of either "it is to be understood almost indifferently and conjointly of both." Pursuing this imagery to its conclusion, Isaac then speaks of each member of the Church: "Every faithful soul, spouse of the Word of God, mother, daughter and sister of Christ is understood to be a virgin with her own form of fertility. This is said of the whole Church, more particularly of Mary and individually of the faithful soul by the Wisdom of God himself, the Father's Word".

It is given to evangelists, bearers of the Good News to bring to others what they themselves have been given to believe and live by. To do it we need not only the charismatic gift of prophecy, we also need what is called the gift of faith.

THE CHARISMATIC GIFT OF FAITH

The word 'faith' has two meanings in the language of Catholic doctrine. The first use of the word refers to what we call one of the 'three theological virtues': faith hope and charity. In this sense of the word, faith means that response to God's holy word which is absolutely necessary for any personal relationship with him.

Without this faith there is no salvation. This is not the faith I refer to here.

The word 'faith' is also used to speak of one of those special gifts of the Spirit we call charisms. "To one is given through the Spirit the utterance of wisdom and to another the utterance of knowledge according to the same Spirit to another faith by the same Spirit, to another gifts of healing" etc.[23] (Before going any further, just remember that, like the eight Beatitudes, to be granted one does not mean you cannot be granted the others as well!)

St. Cyril of Jerusalem, a fourth century bishop, has something to say on the subject. We have already seen how catechumens were prepared to open their hearts to all that the Lord was to offer them in the Sacraments of Christian Initiation. They were also instructed to pray for and to be ready to receive those particular graces that the Spirit has in mind for each person in their individual vocation: the charisms. This is why today, in such exercises as Life in the Spirit seminars, adults once baptised in infancy, are prepared to pray for and open their hearts to what hitherto they took no account of but which is everybody's for the asking: the charismatic gifts they need to fulfil their particular role in the Church's mission. St. Cyril told his catechumens that the charism of faith which St. Paul mentions in his list of spiritual gifts is what Jesus was talking about when he spoke about moving mountains, mustard seeds and mulberry bushes.

In the Gospel according to Mark, the disciples, with astonishment, draw Jesus' attention to the fig tree that withered at his word. Jesus replied, "Have faith in God. I tell you solemnly if anyone says to this mountain, 'Get up and throw yourself into the sea', with no hesitation in his heart but believing that what he says will happen, it will be done for him. I tell you therefore, everything you ask and pray for, believe that you have it already and it will be yours."[24]

In the Gospel according to Matthew, the disciples, having failed to heal the epileptic boy asked why they were unable to cast out the demon. Jesus replied, "Because you have little faith. I tell you solemnly if your faith were the size of a mustard seed you could say to this mountain, 'Move from here to there' and it would move; nothing would be impossible for you."[25]

In the Gospel according to Luke, "The apostles said to the Lord, 'Increase our faith.' The Lord replied, 'Were your faith the size of a mustard seed you could say to this mulberry tree, 'Be uprooted and planted in the sea' and it would obey you."[26]

St. Cyril compared the strength of such faith to the unimaginable energy contained in the mustard seed. Referring to the Lord's words elsewhere, he taught his catechumens, "Now a mustard seed is small in size but its energy thrusts it upwards with the force of fire. Small are its roots, great the spread of its boughs and once it is fully grown the birds of the air find shelter in its branches. So too, in a flash faith can produce the most wonderful effects in the soul."[27] Here the bishop seems to be referring to the soul of the person granted this gift. However, I believe that it is this very gift which empowers the bearer of God's holy word to have so powerful an effect on the soul of another.

I have to say that I do not honestly believe that Jesus was much interested in moving mountains to further the Kingdom of God but he was passionately interested in moving much greater objects: obstinate human hearts. It was said of Jesus, "Who is this man that he forgives sins?" Well, we believe this man sent others to forgive sins in his name. We should also believe that he sent his witnesses with the power to speak the Word that reaches the innermost depths of their listeners, where "the soul is divided from the spirit, the bone from the marrow." Only faith in the indefatigable power of God's Will to establish his reign where as yet it has not come about makes us an apt instrument to share Christ's mission.

St.Cyril says, "Illuminated by faith, *(the soul)* gazes at the glory of God as far as human nature allows and ranging beyond the boundaries of the universe it has a vision, before the consummation of all things, of the judgement and of God making good the rewards he promised".[28] Imagine the transforming vision of what is happening to a person on whom it dawns that, in the human words being addressed to him, the Living God is personally calling him to salvation in Christ. This is what I mean when I say that the work of evangelisation needs people alive with this charism of faith. They are made capable of doing, in the name and power of Christ himself, what is quite beyond all human power. Is it any wonder that St. Cyril admonished those preparing to move from simply being listeners of the Word to become sharers in the Church's apostolic mission, "As far as it depends on you then, cherish the first gift of faith which leads you to God and you will then receive the higher gift which no effort of yours can reach, no powers of yours attain."[29]

Chapter Six

To the glory of His name

It seems to me the very greatest honour that the Lord Jesus should entrust to us the honour of his holy name. To want to be faithful to this trust must be our greatest desire. Once we become conscious of the fact that, by our calling and empowerment in the Spirit we are part of the Mystery of Faith, we shall want to share with all whose lives we touch the great gift which is ours. We are empowered by the Sacraments of Christian Initiation that make us all members of the Body of Christ and the free or charismatic gifts of the Spirit given us individually.

While all the charismatic gifts are of God and all are necessary for the building up of the Church, some are more necessary and therefore, we may say, more important than others. However, the importance of any particular gift must never be judged by how extraordinary or spectacular it appears to our human judgement. How easily we fall into this mistake. The Council teaches, "Whether charisms be very remarkable or more simple and widely diffused, they are to be received with thanksgiving and consolation since they are fitting and useful for the needs of the Church".[1] Every one of us is offered them; not all of us realise this or have welcomed them. Even when we know we have been given them, some of us fail to make use of them. We more easily rely on our natural gifts knowable to us from experience as to their source and their effects.

Although the effects of the charisms can be the object of our senses, their source is not. Their source is the Holy Spirit whose presence in us is the object of faith. This is why great discernment is needed as to whether they are genuinely of the Spirit or not. Should a dispute arise in the community of faith as to their genuineness or usefulness, this is where the institutional and the charismatic gifts meet for, ultimately, 'discernment' is precisely the gift of the episcopate.

This being so, the Council goes on, "Extraordinary gifts are not to be rashly desired nor is it from them that the fruits of apostolic labours are to be presumptuously expected".[2] Like the sacraments, charisms do not operate automatically like slot machines delivering the goods by pressing the right button. The gifts of God do not by-pass labour in the vineyard; they make it possible. They enable us to work fruitfully. In this sense one must be confident that apostolic work undertaken in the power of the Spirit will produce its fruit. The grace of God acting through human beings on other humans may in fact be very ordinary in the sense that it is not uncommon; even so, however ordinary, it is still most wonderful. What is foolish is to imagine we already know what fruit there will be or that we shall correctly discern it when it appears.

GIFTS OF HOLINESS, GIFTS OF SERVICE

In order to appreciate precisely what 'charism' means and how 'charismatic gifts' are needed for mission, a little bit of traditional Catholic theology on the subject will be of great help. In their understanding of God's grace in our lives, theologians make a distinction between those graces which enable us to become holy people and those which are given for the service of others. If you are interested, these are the Latin terms for them:

Gratia gratum faciens – that gift of relationship with God we call 'sanctifying grace' together with those movements of the Spirit prompting us to virtue which we call 'actual graces', terms some of us learned in our childhood catechesis.

Gratia gratis data – gifts that are nothing to do with our personal holiness but gifts that enable us to serve the needs of others.

It can be argued that we become holy only by fulfilling our Christian calling and so we should become better people by using our charisms to fulfil our vocation. This is surely true. However, we can understand why theologians make a distinction between the two. It is eloquently illustrated in the story that used to do the rounds in Welsh non-conformist chapels about the new minister. "Have you heard him? Powerful in prayer – but what a liar!" I know from my own experience of a person whose life was turned around by the preaching of someone who later turned out to be a swindler and paedophile.

It is foolish to assume when we see the charisms at work that we are in the presence of very holy people or to argue that somebody must be a holy person otherwise they would not have been given spiritual gifts. Some people, immature in their spiritual development, suffer greatly, especially in Charismatic circles, asking themselves, "Why do I not have the gift that so-and-so has. I must not be a very good person" All this reveals is that we still do not believe that God's grace is his free, unearned gift. It shows we are still operating within a works and wages religion. Some graces are given for our personal salvation others are given us to minister to others; neither have been earned.

SEEN AND UNSEEN

Just as we bring discernment to the difference between personal sanctity and gifts of service, so we must be very wary of judging what is important and unimportant in the service we are called to give. St. Paul had a mission which continues to bear fruit in countless millions of lives We may admire the extraordinary work of St. Francis Xavier in foreign lands or St. Vincent de Paul in his own land. We may marvel at the extent of the influence St. Teresa of Avila and Mother Teresa of Calcutta continue to have after their deaths. Dazzled perhaps, and bringing a very human judgement to our divine calling, we may take refuge in a phoney, 'Lord I am not worthy' mentality imagining that because the number of people whose lives we seem to touch is more limited, our mission is less important. I see this as a great blindness, subjecting to human wisdom the Mystery of Faith.

Important? To whom is what we think so little, unimportant? How dare we, sent by him who describing himself as the good shepherd, ready to seek out but one lost sheep, hold our mission in so little esteem? If the Lord has it in mind that one should share faith with no more than one person, spouse, son, daughter or friend is this something little thing to him? Once we realise that we are part of the great Sacrament of Salvation the Lord has set up in the world, how can we think that the value of what we have to share can be measured by the number of people with whom, in God's providence, it is given us to share it? Not only our life, but the significance of what we do is hidden from our sight, "in Christ, in God."

What if it had been St. Andrew's sole mission in life to introduce his brother to Jesus of Nazareth, would that not have been a 'tiny' mission but with untold, hidden consequences? St. Monica saw the answer to her prayers for her son Augustine, and died some months later. She famously said, as is quoted on so many memorial cards, "This only I ask, that you remember me at the altar of God wherever you may be".[3] Because the person to whom she was speaking became a priest and bishop people easily imagine she was referring to his priestly ministry at the altar. Actually, she was speaking to her two sons, one of whom never became a priest and the other, of whose future, when she died, she had no idea. She accomplished the mission entrusted to her with no idea of its consequences for the future of the Western Church. When I write of our being prophets through our anointing in the Spirit, and say that prophets are not given a vision of the future but a command to address the present moment, Monica is an example of what I mean.

There can be no doubt that God's call to Augustine was given through Monica, his mother. What God actually had in mind for Augustine, she had no idea of nor did she need to know in order to fulfil all that was asked of her; she simply fulfilled her calling as she understood it. She never knew, in this life, that through her, God was calling into the service of Christ's Gospel a man whose teaching would resound for fifteen hundred years after his death and which shows no signs of losing its authority even now. A good indication of this is that of all the Fathers of the Church and subsequent voices in the church's tradition quoted daily in the Church's Office of Readings, the teachings of St. Augustine, son of Monica, account for at least forty percent of the tradition. That is an amazing legacy. It was brought about through the prayer and witness of someone who was never gifted to give this ministry herself but who was gifted to give the church the minister. It is a wonderful example of that plodding fidelity that characterises so much of the church's mission.

In this matter I have long been impressed by an insight of Thornton Wilder in his book 'The Bridge of San Luis Rey'. One of his fictional characters, Madre Maria del Pilar sees that an extraordinary apostolate she has instigated will not continue after her death because the young woman she has been grooming as her successor had been killed when the bridge crashed. He says that having given up her own vision for its future, "she had an idol torn from her heart" and realised that "it seemed to be sufficient for Heaven that for a while in Peru a disinterested love had flowered and faded."[4] This is the 'holy indifference' written about in the tradition of Christian spirituality. We must embrace the gift to do what the Lord wants done here and now; as to its significance for the future, we may leave that to Him.

Every year in our worship, the Church celebrates the grace of God in all his saints. It recognises that it is only through the labours of real men and women now dead that the Church exists today. Some carried out their mission in ways that were so public that the fruits of their labours are manifest for all to see. With others, the fruits may be evident, but the labours are not. Communities of faith exist throughout the world but who, by the grace of God, is responsible for their existence? Who, by the grace of God, nourished and sustained them? Yes, we know the names of a handful but for the rest?

We believe that among the whole people sent by God as bearers of the Good News, the Twelve were given a foundational commission that continues for ever in Christ's Church in the heir to the Twelve, the College of Bishops. However, what has history recorded of their labours? Apart from pious legends, what does anyone really know of the work undertaken by Andrew, Philip, Bartholomew, Matthew, Thomas, Jude or Matthias? Nothing. Even so, on their feast days, the Church sings of them, "their word goes forth through all the earth". It offers God praise in these words, for it knows that its entire history springs from the faithful work of this company. However in the same act of praise, it honours them with words the psalm applies to the sun and the moon in their silent testimony to God's glory:

> "No speech, no word, no voice is heard
> Yet their span extends through all the earth,
> Their word to the utmost bounds of the world."[5]

This is a beautiful confession that although human history has recorded nothing of their labour we can praise God for the evidence of its fruit for it believes that the worship it celebrates even today is 'the faith that comes to us from the Apostles'.[6]

Human history may record nothing of our lives and labours but if they have been carried out in the Spirit they are known to Heaven. In this context Julian of Norwich speaks most touchingly about God's regard for our service. She sees the soul that has reached its destination hearing the words of the Lord, "I thank thee for thy service and for thy travail and especially in thy youth." The joy these words must bring she speaks of as "so high and so worshipful that it will seem to him that it filleth him, though there were no other bliss. For methought that all the pain and travail that might be suffered by all men living could not have deserved the thanking that one man shall have who willingly has served his God".[7] The idea of the Lord, out of whose bounty everything springs, thanking us for what we have done causes a blush in the depths of my heart.

The Lord says that anyone who so much as gives a cup of water in his name will not be without his reward. No human gesture that puts another human being before oneself is without meaning or purpose in the coming of God's Kingdom. Where disciples of Christ act in this way, moved to go beyond themselves precisely because they are disciples, then Christ acts through them and is able through any word or gesture of this kind to touch the heart of another. This is charismatic Christianity at work. It is the steady plod of the Christian life that makes up ninety-nine percent of any life whether that is the life of an individual, a community or the whole sweep of human history.

BAPTISM IN THE SPIRIT

In ancient times, when catechumens experienced the full power of the Sacraments of Christian Initiation, they experienced also the power of the charismatic gifts. This is the grace which today is called 'Baptism in the Spirit'. In their experience of the Sacraments, they felt the power of the Spirit with whom they were newly filled. Indeed it was that they might *experience* the effect of God's grace in their lives that the Catechumenate instilled in them 'a profound sense of the mysteries'. People baptised in infancy having only a cerebral knowledge of Catholic doctrine may well lack this profound sense. By prayer and a new conversion they can become disposed to receive a new outpouring of the Spirit, awakening them to this sense of the mystery. Only when one has chosen to awake, for we are not inert, inanimate tools but partners with the Spirit can we 'burst into flame'. It is never too late to wake up to what is ours for the asking, for the living Spirit of God is sovereign, supremely free to act as and when he will in the life of every member of the Church. We have but to know he longs to suffuse us with his power and answer longing with longing. We have but to yield to the giver of all that is needed, to live fully our life in Christ and fulfil our mission.

I have kept on insisting that the mystery we have been called to share in and give witness to is the object of our faith, not our feelings, emotions or reason. But this does not mean that experience is not involved or must be ignored.

"Whether any one of us has ever been, as we say, 'aware' of the presence of God or not, it is certain with the certainty of faith that he is present to us *in some way* at this moment since, were this not so, we should not even be here. It is also equally certain, on the same grounds, that we all of us stand in some definite relationship to that divine presence, whether we have any inkling of what that relationship is or not. God at least knows what it is, and all traditional theologians would believe that there will always be *some things* about that relationship that we can never know for certain in this world. On the other hand, we do know for certain that God wishes that relationship to come alive *at our end*, as something that can be humanly known and responded to."[8]

This 'coming alive' of all that we said we believed is known as 'Baptism in the Spirit'. That it accompanied the celebration of the Sacraments of Initiation in ancient days is testified to by St Cyprian, who was to become the martyr bishop of Carthage. He was baptised in his middle thirties in the year 246 and later wrote to a friend, Donatus, about his life-changing experience of Easter Night:
"I promised to share with you the grace God in his great mercy has shown me and to tell you as simply as I can what I experienced since I was baptized.

"Until that time I was still living in the dark, knowing nothing of my true life... Frankly, I could not see how a person could cast off all his fallen nature and be changed in heart and soul while he still lived in the same body as before. How is it possible, I asked myself, to change the habits of a lifetime instantaneously?... Is every species of temptation suddenly to lose its force?... These were my thoughts... I despaired of ever being any better. But at last I made up my mind to ask for baptism.

"I went down into those life-giving waters and all the stains of my past were washed away. I committed my life to the Lord; he cleansed my heart and filled me with his Holy Spirit. I was born again, a new man... I found I could do things that had previously been impossible. I saw that as long as I had been living according to my lower nature I was at the mercy of sin and my course was set for death; but that by living according to my new birth in the Holy Spirit I had already begun to share God's eternal life. You know as well as I do what sins I died to at that moment, just as you know the gifts the Holy Spirit gave me along with my new life. I have no desire to boast but it is surely right to thank God for his free gift... All our power for good is God's gift... The amount of grace we receive is measured by the faith with which we appropriate it... How tremendous is this freedom and the spiritual power the Lord has given us!"[9]

St. Ireneus lived a generation earlier than St. Cyprian. He saw that the glory of God is revealed in his restoring mankind to his image and likeness in Jesus Christ crucified and risen. He saw this glory manifested in mankind sharing the divine life through the outpouring of the Holy Spirit. "The glory of God is man fully alive and the life of man is the vision of God".[10] It is this vision of who and what we have become by answering our Christian calling that I have wanted to share in this book. In the end is our beginning and as I reach the end of these reflections, I return to that initial moment of awe from which sprang my own adult discipleship and apostolate in the presence of him who says, "I am the alpha and the omega, the beginning and the end".

WORSHIPPING THE MYSTERY

Comparing the Mystery of Faith to which the Gospel calls us with the sacred signs of God's presence in the Old Testament, I quoted the Letter to the Hebrews. Having made his point the writer gives a warning not to treat so great a gift lightly for to do so, as we would say, is 'playing with fire'. "We should offer worship pleasing to God with reverence and awe. For God is a consuming fire."[11] If however we approach the mystery not to take or leave it at our pleasure but to contemplate with worship, we shall find that we burn but we burn with a flame that does not devour us.

The Bible tells a story at the very beginning of Israel's history in which I find an image of God's one purpose in all creation. This purpose was ultimately revealed in Him who is Emmanuel, God with us, and who gathers to himself God's beloved creation, establishing in the world a visible sign of this divine work.

It is said of Moses that while pasturing sheep he caught sight of a bush which, "though on fire, was not consumed".[12] The R.S.V. reads,"The Lord seeing that he turned aside...." The New American Bible says, "When God saw him coming over to look at it more closely," the Lord addressed him. Both translations suggest the ephemeral nature of any moment of grace and the unknowable possibilities it offers or the immeasurable consequences of ignoring it. "Oh that today, you would listen to his voice!" If we do permit the Word of God to break into our self-created world, who knows what will be the result.

The bush that was aflame without being devoured suggests to me a vision of Salvation History's ultimate purpose. Of this purpose, the Church is the promise and pledge of its fulfillment: the concrete reality of physical creation, penetrated by the Divine Presence.

In Jesus, God is forever united with his beloved creation in the mystery of the Incarnation. I see this mystery represented in the earth-rooted bush ablaze with heavenly fire.

In Jesus, crucified and risen, God has destroyed the power of all that would separate his creation from himself and bound himself to his creation in an everlasting covenant. This is prefigured in the ephemeral bush ablaze with an undying flame.

In Christ, head and members, God's creation over which the Spirit has hovered from the beginning, awaiting the appropriate moment to descend is now suffused by the Spirit. All this I see prefigured in the bush that is not destroyed by being aflame.

This mystery exists, here and now, on the fringes of our consciousness. That we may awaken to its reality, it needs only that we 'turn aside' from what seems more real, more pressing, more important to us. Should we do so, there is an image far more prosaic than Moses' burning bush which captured my imagination and which may impress upon us the mystical reality of what faith confronts us with.

Reflecting on the burning bush I remembered from my childhood how gas mantles worked. The gas mantle is a very fragile artefact. One slight injury and it is no longer fit for purpose. In this it is like human nature itself. But God, taking this fragile creation to himself, has restored it, repairing the damage of sin's injury. It may thrill us to believe that God in Christ forgives our sins and heals our wounds. But it may also be that in coming thus far on our faith journey we still have no idea of the wonders that lie beyond. This is our situation if we are catechumens or baptised persons still living in that period of our Christian formation I have described as being psychologically a catechumen. To be freed from sin is but to begin the journey into the Mystery of Faith.

The repaired gas mantle, no matter how awesome the work of restoration, has not yet begun to fulfil its purpose. This it does only when filled with gas. Through Jesus crucified and risen, God has restored in us his image and likeness, the necessary preliminary to our being filled with the Spirit - (in our Anglo Saxon words, ghost, geist, gas). But, the gas must be lit! This happens when we 'turn aside' from what, hitherto we have assumed our Catholic Christian life to be all about and receive a new sense of the mystery in which we are involved. This is the grace known as 'Baptism in the Spirit' By this grace we may begin to realise that the restored gas mantle is burning – yet anything but destroyed by the flame.

Once upon a time only Moses was called and sent but in this last age his prayer has been answered: the whole people is now filled with the Spirit, called and sent.

This is the vision Catholic Christian tradition offers everyone wishing to respond to God's call. It is my vision of the Body of Christ on earth in whose life and mission we are called to share. It is a promise for all created reality, when human history has run its course, and God is 'all in all'. It is a vision of living 'through him, with him and in him' who stands in the midst of his church and says, "I am the alpha and the omega, the first and the last, the beginning and the end".[14]

Notes

Preface: Sharing what we have been given

1. Luke 16.12
2. www.catholic-hierarchy.org
3. 2nd Vatican Council, 'Lumen Gentium', articles 13 and 23
4. 'Life and Liturgy' Louis Bouyer p.4, et seq. Sheed and Ward, 1956
5. Celebration of the Lord's Passion, General Intercessions, No.8
6. Confessions of St. Augustine, Bk.9, 10.
7. Bl. John XXIII, Opening address to 2nd Vatican Council,11th. Oct. 1962
8. Introduction, Rite of Christian Initiation of Adults, no. 34 cf. 56
9. Summa Theologica, 1 q.19, a.2
10. 1 John 1. 3-4
11. John 4.14
12. John 7.38-39

Chapter 1: My own experience of being called and sent

1. Eucharistic Prayer, No.4. Roman Missal.
2. 'On the Predestination of the Saints', Chap 15; quoted in the Office of Readings; Friday of Week 13
3. Mark 12. 28-34
4. Pope Paul VI, in 1975 'Evangelii Nuntiandi' 46
5. St. Jerome, Letter no. 148
6. 'Sacrae Thologiae Summa' vol IV, p.639. BAC Madrid, 1962, 4th edition
7. 1 Pet. 3.15
8. Rom. 16.7
9. A Path from Rome: An Autobiography.' A. Kenny, 1986.Oxford Univ. Press
10. 'Asking the Fathers', p.3, Aelred Squire, Morehouse-Barlow. Co. New York, 1973

11. Pope Paul VI, Opening discourse, 2nd Session, Vatican II, para.17; 29th Sept,1963
12. Pope John Paul II, Pentecost homily, 1998

Chapter 2: Come, follow me

1. Matt.7.7.
2. John 1. 39.
3. John. 5.37-40
4. John.1.50-51
5. Gen. 28. 10-15
6. Isaiah
7. Psalm 107.14
8. John
9. John 20.28
10. John 11.16
11. John 20, 30-31
12. John 20, 16
13. John 20.21
14. Exultet, Easter Vigil
15. John 14.6

Chapter 3: Learning to be a disciple

1. 'Four Quartets – East Coker' by T.S. Eliot, Faber Paperbacks
2. Confessions of St. Augustine, Bk.7, 27.
3. Colossians.3.3
4. Sermons of St. Augustine, No.179
5. St. Jerome, Commentary on Isaiah, Prologue
6. Daniel 3 26-45 (verses) used in The Office of Readings, Tuesday, Wk 2
7. St. Ambrose, On the Mysteries (No. 1-7; SC 25, 156-158)
8. Luke, 24.32
9. Pope Pius XI, Letter (October 17, 1926), to the Piedmontese Bishops.

10. Summa Theologica, 3a pars, qu.62. art. 6
11. 1 Cor.3, 16-17
12. Col. 3.3.
13. 'A Shewing of God's Love' chap. 4

Chapter 4: Christian Initiation

1. Mark 7, 34
2. Isaiah 6, 9-10
3. 'From Darkness to Light' Anne Field O.S.B., p.208, note 32
4. Heb. 12,18-24
5. 'Lumen Gentium', art. 1
6. John 20.28
7. 1 Cor. 1 2

Chapter 5: As the Father sent me

1. 'Lumen Gentium', art. 12
2. Is.61.1.ff
3. Lk. 4.43
4. Matthew 13,6
5. 1 King 18.21
6. R.C.I.A. Gen. Intro. no. 75 para 1
7. Heb.1.1. 2
8. Cor. 5,20
9. Rite of Infant Baptism.
10. Matt. 7, 16
11. Matt. 10, 19-20
12. Num.11.29
13. Heb. 4:12-13
14. Matt. 28,20
15. John 15. 5
16. John 14 12

17. Tract 6, quoted in Office of Readings, Friday, 13th. Week
18. John 1.15
19. Sermon 293, quoted in Office of Readings, 3rd Sunday of Advent
20. Prologue of the Commentary of Isaiah, No.1,2.
21 2 Cor. 4.7
22. Sermon 51
23. 1 Cor. 12: 4-11
24. Mk.11: 20-25
25. Matt. 17: 19-20
26. Lk. 17: 5-6
27. Cat.5, De fide et symbolo, quoted in Office of Readings, Wed. Wk.31
28. op cit.
29. op cit.

Chapter 6: To the glory of His name

1. 'Lumen Gentium'. art. 12
2. Op cit.
3. Confessions of St. Augustine, Lib.9, 11
4. 'The Bridge of San Luis Rey' p. 90, Thornton Wilder, Penguin Books
5. Ps 19. 4
6. Eucharistic Prayer No.1; Roman Missal
7. 'A Shewing of God's Love', chap., 9
8. Author's italics. 'Asking the Fathers', Aelred Squire. p.13
9. 'Epistola ad Donatum de gratia Dei,' quoted in 'From Darkness to Light', Anne Field, O.S.B. P.190, Servant Books.
10. 'Against the Heresies', 4.20.7
11. Heb.12.28-29
12. Exodus 3.3
13. I Cor. 15, 34
14. Rev. 22,13

Further copies of this book
can be obtained from

Goodnews Books
Upper Level
St. John's Church Complex
296 Sundon Park Road
Luton,Beds, UK, LU3 3AL

01582 571011
orders@goodnewsbooks.net
www.goodnewsbooks.net